El Alamein 1942

The Turning of the Tide

Campaign • 158

El Alamein 1942

The Turning of the Tide

Ken Ford · Illustrated by Howard Gerrard

Series editor Lee Johnson

First published in Great Britain in 2005 by Osprey Publishing,
Midland House, West Way, Botley, Oxford OX2 0PH, UK
44-02 23rd St, Suite 219, Long Island City, NY 11101, USA
Email: info@ospreypublishing.com

Transferred to digital print on demand 2011

First published 2005
5th impression 2010

Printed and bound by PrintOnDemand-Worldwide.com Peterborough, UK

A CIP catalogue record for this book is available from the British Library

ISBN: 978 1 84176 867 0

The author, Ken Ford, has asserted his right under the Copyright, Designs and Patents Act, 1988,
to be identified as the Authors of this Work.

Design by The Black Spot
Index by Alan Thatcher
Maps by the Map Studio
3D bird's-eye views by The Black Spot
Originated by The Electronic Page Company, Cwmbran, UK
Typeset in Helvetica Neue and ITC New Baskerville

Acknowledgements
I should like to express my gratitude to Pier Paolo Battistelli and to LtCol Filippo Cappellano for the help they gave with regard to
photographs of the Italian forces of Panzerarmee Afrika. Thanks also go to author Robin Neillands for providing me with modern
photographs of the battlefield.

Artist's note
Readers may care to note that the original paintings from which the colour plates in this book were prepared are available for
private sale. All reproduction copyright whatsoever is retained by the Publisher. Enquiries should be addressed to:

Howard Gerrard, 11 Oaks Road, Tenterden, Kent, TN30 6RD, UK

The Publishers regret that they can enter into no correspondence upon this matter.

The Woodland Trust
Osprey Publishing is supporting the Woodland Trust, the UK's leading woodland conservation charity, by funding the
dedication of trees.

www.ospreypublishing.com

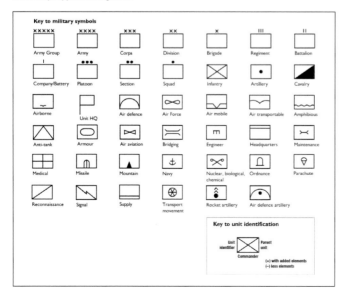

CONTENTS

ORIGINS OF THE BATTLE

The three battles which took place in the desert to the south of the isolated railway station of El Alamein in 1942 marked the climax of Hitler's plan to wrest Egypt from the British. His goal of seizing the Suez Canal and opening the Middle East to Axis forces had to be abandoned when his forces were soundly beaten. The success of these three actions transferred the initiative back to the British and precipitated the collapse of Generalfeldmarschall Erwin Rommel's Panzerarmee Afrika, forcing it into a long retreat across North Africa which eventually ended in its complete annihilation in Tunisia the following year. The final battle of El Alamein was a turning point in the war and was the last signal achievement gained by the British before American troops entered the conflict. Prime Minister Winston Churchill later claimed that before Alamein the British Army had not gained a major victory; after Alamein it did not suffer a major defeat.

The Desert War had begun as a colonial skirmish in September 1940 when Italian forces crossed the border from Libya into Egypt. The garrison of 36,000 British under Gen Wavell faced 215,000 Italians led by General Marshal Graziani. Undaunted by the overwhelming odds, Wavell's forces attacked the invaders and threw them out, following up the success with belligerent moves under LtGen O'Connor which pushed the Italians back across the whole of Cyrenaica to El Agheila. During the course of the final part of the advance, a British force of one armoured division and one infantry division completely destroyed an

The three architects of the victory at El Alamein together in Egypt in August 1942. From left to right: Gen Sir Harold Alexander (C-in-C Middle East), Winston Churchill (British Prime Minister) and LtGen Sir Bernard Montgomery (Commander Eighth Army). (IWM E15905)

MajGen Gatehouse, Commander 10th Armoured Division, in his Crusader command tank prior to the start of Operation *Lightfoot*, the attack phase of the battle of Alamein. (IWM E17616)

enemy army of ten divisions, capturing 130,000 Italians, for the loss of 1,928 men killed, wounded and missing.

At this point, the British government decided to hold Cyrenaica with the smallest possible force while the rest of the army and air force concentrated in Egypt prior to a move to Greece to help stem the Axis troops who were trying to take over the country. Gen Wavell was against the move reasoning that a further advance through Libya could capture the port of Tripoli and evict Mussolini's Fascists from North Africa completely. He was overruled and valuable troops were sent to Greece, only to be unceremonially evicted by the Germans with considerable casualties.

Gen Erwin Rommel then arrived in North Africa on 12 February 1941 and, with a small force of German troops to stiffen Italian resolve, proceeded to push the depleted British force right back to the Egyptian border, leaving just the surrounded garrison in Tobruk as the only British left in Libya. This small German contribution to the Italian-sponsored campaign was gradually enlarged by new arrivals and eventually became the famed Afrika Korps comprising of 15th and 21st Panzer Divisions. It then became the backbone of the Italian–German army for the rest of the Desert War.

The British launched two attempts to push Rommel back and relieve Tobruk during the early part of 1941; both failed. Wavell was then replaced by Gen Claude Auchinleck as C-in-C Middle East. His forces in Egypt were designated British Eighth Army and placed under the command of Gen Alan Cunningham. In November 1941 Cunningham launched Operation *Crusader* against Rommel. It was not a great success. There followed a good deal of heavy fighting and much advance and retreat by both sides. Tobruk was relieved and Rommel at one point was pushed right back to El Agheila in Tripolitania where he first started. During the fighting, Auchinleck lost faith in the performance of Eighth Army's commander and replaced him with LtGen Neil Ritchie. At this point Auchinleck's position was weakened by the removal of British and Australian formations to the Far East to counter Japan's

EIGHTH ARMY RETREAT

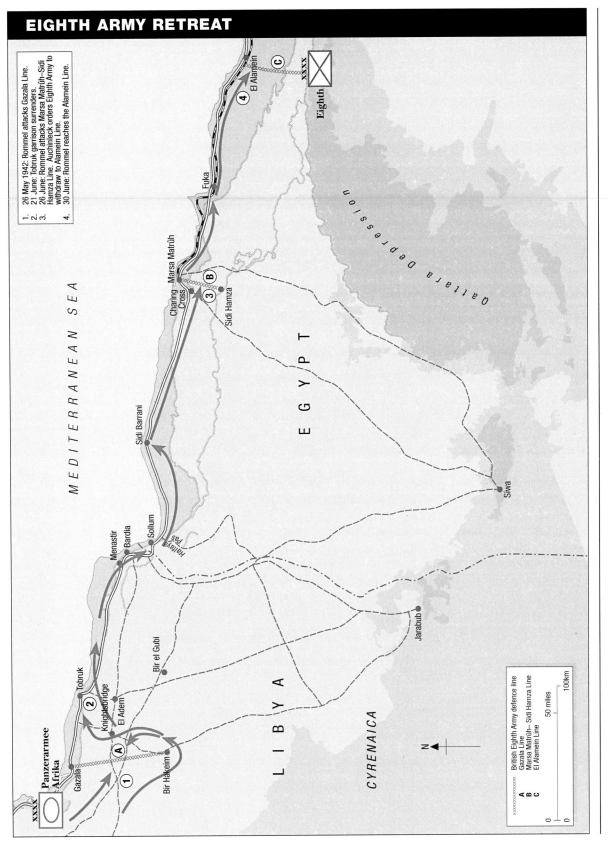

1. 26 May 1942: Rommel attacks Gazala Line.
2. 21 June: Tobruk garrison surrenders.
3. 26 June: Rommel attacks Marsa Matrûh–Sidi Hamza Line. Auchinleck orders Eighth Army to withdraw to Alamein Line.
4. 30 June: Rommel reaches the Alamein Line.

Panzerarmee Afrika

MEDITERRANEAN SEA

LIBYA

CYRENAICA

EGYPT

Qattara Depression

Gazala
Bir Hakeim
Tobruk
Knightsbridge
El Adem
Bir el Gubi
Menastir
Bardia
Sollum
Halfaya Pass
Sidi Barrani
Marsa Matrûh
Charing Cross
Sidi Hamza
Fuka
El Alamein
Eighth
Siwa
Jarabub

N

British Eighth Army defence line
A Gazala Line
B Marsa Matrûh– Sidi Hamza Line
C El Alamein Line

0   50 miles
0   100km

9

entry into the war. Rommel, on the other hand, had withdrawn his forces intact and was reinforced early in 1942 by 90th Light Division, ready to resume the offensive. Axis forces attacked eastwards once again on 21 January and pushed the British back to a prepared line running south from Gazala.

From early February until mid May there was a lull in the fighting while the two sides built up their forces in preparation for a renewed offensive. Rommel struck first on 26 May and over the next few weeks out-fought and out-manoeuvred Ritchie's army. During the protracted struggle Eighth Army lost 50,000 men and was forced into retreat, streaming back in some disarray towards the Egyptian border. Tobruk was abandoned along with quantities of supplies and equipment. A jubilant Rommel pressed hard on the heels of the British withdrawal, intent on driving straight though to Cairo.

On 23 June the battered Eighth Army took up a position just inside Egypt at Mersa Matruh. Complete defeat became a distinct possibility. Auchinleck realized that drastic steps had to be taken to prevent the enemy reaching the Nile Delta and capturing the Suez Canal, for once Axis troops were across the waterway, Hitler might be tempted to send forces south from the Caucasus to link up with them and then move on the oil fields of Iraq and Persia.

With few features standing above the flat desert landscape, a British officer uses the height of his Marmon Herrington armoured vehicle to improve his view of the enemy. (IWM E14068)

Auchinleck at this point removed Ritchie and placed himself in personal command of Eighth Army. His overriding consideration was to keep the army intact, even if it meant giving up Egypt. After a two-day running battle at Mursa Matruh, the withdrawal continued to a half-prepared defensive line at El Alamein. To the rear of this, just before the delta, he ordered more defences to be dug and asked his planners to consider how further withdrawals into Palestine or south towards the Sudan could be effected. Auchinleck planned to stop Rommel's advance at El Alamein. Failing that, he would try again on a makeshift line before the Delta. Whatever happened, he would not allow Eight Army to be overwhelmed; it must be kept intact as a fighting force to continue the struggle with the enemy, wherever the next battlefield might happen to be.

British Eighth Army, exhausted by its hurried retreat, was in position on the El Alamein line by 30 June. Following close behind, the equally weary advance units of Rommel's Panzerarmee Afrika brushed up against it the same day. Both sides now squared up to each other across kilometres of barren desert and quickly prepared for a decisive showdown: one aiming for victory, the other merely trying to stop the rot. The fighting that followed, however, did not end in a decisive showdown, for it took three separate battles before a result could be declared.

The first of these battles is usually recognized as being First Alamein, although many modern historians take exception to this title, believing that Gen Auchinleck's successful attempt to stop Rommel was no more than two weeks of disparate actions fought by two exhausted armies each trying to regain the upper hand. The second battle was Alam Halfa, Rommel's last, unsuccessful operation to get past a revitalized Eighth Army into Egypt. By then things had changed; Auchinleck had gone, replaced by Gen Harold Alexander, and Eighth Army had a new commander, LtGen Bernard Montgomery. Alam Halfa marked the beginning of the turnaround in British fortunes: Rommel was stopped and the initiative passed to Montgomery. Then, after both sides had spent almost two months in preparation, came the battle known to the world as El Alamein: Montgomery's greatest triumph, when Rommel was finally defeated in a stand-up fight.

CHRONOLOGY

1942

26 May Rommel attacks British line at Gazala and, after a long, drawn-out battle, breaks through Gen Ritchie's Eighth Army.

14 June A general retreat by Eighth Army to the Marsa Matruh–Sidi Hamza line is ordered. The 2nd South African Division is left to hold Tobruk.

21 June Tobruk falls.

25 June Auchinleck removes Ritchie and takes over direct command of Eighth Army.

26 June Auchinleck cancels his order for a stand on the Marsa Matruh–Sidi Hamza line and instructs his formations to fall back to the El Alamein line, but the enemy is already in contact and a two-day battle of disengagement is fought by the almost-surrounded British X and XIII Corps.

30 June All British forces are withdrawn behind the Alamein positions.

1–3 July Rommel launches an infantry attack against the Alamein 'box' with 90th Light Division and sends his Afrika Korps round its flank. Both attacks fail to dislodge the British.

9 July Rommel attacks in the south of the line with the tanks of 21st Panzer and Littorio Divisions, but fails to make a breakthrough.

10–14 July Australian 9th Division captures Tel el Eisa near the coast and withstands counterattacks against both this salient and the Alamein 'box'.

15–17 July New Zealand Division launches an unsuccessful attack on the Ruweisat Ridge, failing to dislodge the enemy.

21–22 July Combined Australian, New Zealand and South African attack on Rommel's centre is initially successful. However, further countermoves by the enemy eventually drive them back.

26–27 July The Australians begin an attack south-westwards from Tel el Eisa towards the Miteirya Ridge. By this time both sides are well established in defence and tired. The Australian attack fails to shift the enemy and Auchinleck calls a halt. Both he and Rommel realize that further gains are impossible before their forces have rested and replenished their supplies. Both now strengthen their defences and gather for the next attack. This first battle of Alamein has stopped Rommel's advance towards Cairo and saved Egypt.

12 August Montgomery arrives in Egypt to take over Eighth Army. Alexander has already assumed command as C-in-C Middle East in place of Auchinleck.

31 August Rommel launches his final attack to break through the Alamein line.

1–4 September After two days of fighting, Axis forces are unable to get past Montgomery's strong defences about Alam Halfa Ridge and Rommel pulls back his army. His retreat is then hit in the flank by the New Zealand Division, but the counterattack is beaten off with only minimal losses.

September–October Rommel continues to strengthen his defences and Montgomery carries on with the build-up of his forces ready for the showdown battle on the Alamein line.

23 October Montgomery fires the largest artillery barrage yet seen in the war and launches Operation *Lightfoot*. XXX Corps attacks the northern minefields of Rommel's positions and attempts to carve out an area ready for X Corps to force two corridors through the Axis defences.

One of the hazards of the desert, a sand storm, is rolling across the flat terrain and will soon engulf this British officer and his jeep in an impenetrable cloud of grit and choking dust. One such incident disrupted Rommel's initial attack during the first Alamein battle. (IWM E17824)

Welcome supplies, including bread and water, arrive at the *Panzerwerkstattkompanie* (tank repair company) of the 21st Panzer Division's 5th Panzer Regiment. (Bundesarchiv 1011-782-0006-22)

The arrival of Lee and Grant tanks in the desert at last gave the British weapons that could take on the German Panzer IVs on something like parity. The sponson-mounted 75mm gun and the turret-mounted 37mm gun gave it the kind of punch that had been missing in British armour. Illustrated here is the Lee, it differed from the Grant in having a commander's machine gun cupola on the top of the turret. (IWM E14050)

Once through the German line, Monty intends to bring the German armour to battle on his terms. Secondary attacks are also launched in the south by XIII Corps to confuse the enemy.

24–26 October Montgomery's corps in both sectors of the line fail to penetrate the main German defences. In the north the armour of British X Corps is reluctant to advance too far forward of the infantry. Constant urgings by Montgomery fail to galvanize his forces for a supreme effort.

26 October Australian 9th Division begins to carve out a salient around Point 29 in the north and 1st Armoured Division attack Kidney Ridge to the south of the Australian effort.

27 October Rommel launches a counterattack against 1st Armoured Division with his Afrika Korps, but is checked by the British division's anti-tank guns. Similar enemy attacks against the Australians are also turned back.

28–30 October Montgomery now switches his main effort to the north and uses the Australian Division to carve out a salient towards the coast. Rommel counters this move by shifting more of his armour northwards.

LEFT **Troops from Australian 9th Division try to master the workings of a captured Italian 47/32 M25 anti-tank gun. (IWM E16678)**

Italian infantry with their standard infantry anti-tank gun, the 47/32 M35. This gun was built under licence and derived from the Austrian 47mm Böhler gun. No shield was provided as the gun could be broken down into five loads for easy transportation. Its low profile made it difficult to detect in the desert. (IWM RML 627)

1 November Montgomery changes his plans again and decides to throw his main weight into the line south of the Australians in Operation *Supercharge*.

2 November The New Zealand infantry attack on a two-brigade front and break into the German defences. Superb fighting by 9th Armoured Brigade holds open a gap to allow the armour of X Corps to pass through.

3 November A battle of attrition grinds down the enemy defences and they begin to crumble. Cracks open in the line and more and more of Eighth Army's divisions begin to fight their way through.

4 November The Battle of Alamein is won. Axis forces are in retreat, streaming back towards the coast road, heading for the Egyptian border.

8 November Anglo-American forces under Gen Eisenhower land in Morocco and Algeria then move swiftly into Tunisia. Rommel now has an Allied army to his front and rear.

23 November Rommel is back where he started in January 1942 at El Agheila. He plans to make a stand, but then slips away as the British try to outflank his lines. Panzerarmee Afrika is now in full retreat westwards, intending to make a stand on the Mareth Line inside Tunisia.

OPPOSING COMMANDERS

The North African desert was a graveyard of the reputations of many senior British generals, as each in turned failed to bring about a resolute victory. It was the only ground on which Britain was in contact with Axis forces and to this battlefield were sent the best that Britain had to offer. It is therefore not surprising that the Prime Minister became depressed by the continued lack of success of his generals. In June 1942, after almost two years of battle, there should have been some concrete achievements to show for all the fighting, but British Forces were right back where they started and, more to the point, they were in serious trouble. On the enemy side, the array of senior commanders changed little in the Desert War. Those replacements that were sent to North Africa were usually as a result of death, injury or sickness.

BRITISH COMMANDERS

General Sir Claude Auchinleck (1884–1981) had been appointed as Commander-in-Chief Middle East in July 1941, replacing Gen Sir Archibald Wavell, who was sacked after the disastrous attempts to relieve the besieged port of Tobruk. Ulster-born Auchinleck was a product of the colonial Indian Army, having been commissioned into 62nd Punjab Regiment in 1904. He saw action in the First World War in Egypt, Aden and Mesopotamia. After the outbreak of war in 1939, he commanded the British and French troops in northern Norway during the abortive campaign of 1940 and later took up corps and army commands in England before moving east to become C-in-C India. As C-in-C Middle East, Auchinleck had responsibility not only for military events in North Africa, but for the continuing troubles in Palestine, Iraq and Persia. He was a modest man, austere and spartan in his lifestyle, but with a great regard for the welfare of the soldiers in his command. Auchinleck was much admired by his contemporaries and proved himself an able commander when, as head of Eighth Army, he stopped Rommel's headlong charge towards Cairo at First Alamein. Unfortunately, he was not a great communicator and often irritated Churchill with his preoccupation of trying to beat Rommel rather than attending to the Prime Minister's urgings.

By August 1942, Churchill was so unhappy with Auchinleck's performance that he insisted in changes of command being made. Auchinleck was dismissed and replaced by two men: Gen Alexander as C-in-C Middle East and LtGen Montgomery as commander Eighth Army.

General Sir Harold Alexander was born the third son of the Earl of Caledon and was educated at Harrow. He graduated from Sandhurst in 1911 and gained a commission in the Irish Guards. He saw service in the First World War as a battalion commander, during which time he was twice wounded and won both the MC and DSO. Between the wars he served in India and in 1937 at the age of 45 became the youngest major-general in the British Army. He commanded 1st Division in France in 1940 and then I Corps during the evacuation at Dunkirk. He then served in Burma before taking over in the Middle East. Alexander was not recognized as a commander of great strategic ability, but he was a good administrator and diplomat. He had a reputation for surrounding himself with good staff officers of great competence. In North Africa he was more than pleased to leave all strategic and tactical decisions to his army commander.

LtGen Sir Bernard Montgomery (centre) with two of his corps commanders. On the left is LtGen Oliver Leese (XXX Corps) and on the right LtGen Herbert Lumsden (X Corps). (IWM E18416)

LtGen Sir Bernard Montgomery was a thoroughly professional soldier who had made a careful study of his craft in order to develop definite ideas of how war should be conducted. He was born in 1887, the son of a bishop. He left Sandhurst in 1908 and joined the Warwickshire Regiment on the North-West Frontier of India. During the First World War he joined the BEF just after the retreat from Mons in August 1914. He was wounded two months later and awarded the DSO. He ended the war as Chief-of Staff of 47th Division. In the inter-war years he became an instructor at Camberley. At the outbreak of the Second World War he was in command of 3rd Division. He took this formation to France in 1940 and then assumed command of II Corps on the retreat to Dunkirk. For the next two years he rose in rank until he eventually led South-Eastern Army. Montgomery had no doubts about his own ability and was contemptuous of the lack of proficiency in others. He was a difficult man to work for, or to be in command of, and had a number of detractors amongst his fellow officers. Many found him insufferable, but few doubted his competence.

After he had taken over Eighth Army in August 1942, Montgomery sought to replace some of his subordinate commanders with men that he knew. His judgement was usually proved right and many of these men themselves went on to higher command. **LtGen Sir Oliver Leese,** a tank specialist who had instructed at the Quetta Staff College in the 1930s, was brought out to Egypt from the Guards Division to lead XXX Corps. His performance in the desert eventually led to him taking over command of Eighth Army later in the war in Italy. Sometimes Montgomery was wrong in his choice of subordinates as in the case of **LtGen Herbert Lumsden** who was given the command of X Corps. Lumsden had previously commanded 1st Armoured Division and was elevated to corps command on the recommendation of others. X Corps did not perform well during the main battle of El Alamein, where Lumsden and his armoured commanders disagreed with the army commander's use of armour. Montgomery was not best pleased and replaced Lumsden soon after the battle.

The war in the desert produced many fine divisional commanders, the most impressive of which was **LtGen Sir Bernard Freyberg VC**, commander New Zealand 2nd Division. The bravery he showed in the First World War where he won Britain's highest decoration, continued in the desert, for the actions fought by his division won great praise, not least of which came

LtGen Brian Horrocks, Commander XIII Corps. Horrocks was highly regarded by Montgomery and the new Eighth Army commander lost no time in promoting him to corps command. XIII Corps had previously been led by LtGen 'Strafer' Gott who had been Churchill's first choice to take over Eighth Army after Auchinleck, but Gott was killed in an air crash days before he could assume the command. (IWM 16462)

LtGen Sir Bernard Freyberg (centre), commander of New Zealand 2nd Division, greets the Foreign Secretary, Sir Anthony Eden, on his visit to Egypt. (E18781)

from Rommel himself who regarded the New Zealanders as being among the elite of the British Army. Similar regard was given to the other two commanders of Dominion divisions: **LtGen Sir Leslie Morshead** of Australian 9th Division and **MajGen D.H. Pienaar** of South African First Division.

AXIS COMMANDERS

The Axis chain of command in North Africa was rather complex. The theatre was, strictly speaking, an Italian show, with **Marshal Ugo Cavallero** as its Commando Supremo. Cavallero was a veteran of the First World War who had spent a great deal of time in the inter-war years in industry. He was C-in-C East Africa before succeeding Marshal Badoglio as Italian Chief of General Staff in November 1940. Marshal Cavallero reported directly to the Fascist leader Benito Mussolini in Rome. Also in Italy was the veteran Luftwaffe commander **Generalfeldmarschall Albert Kesselring** who was C-in-C of all German forces in the Mediterranean. German and Italian forces in North Africa had been combined, with the overall commander of these troops being **Marshal Ettore Bastico**. The reality was, however, that GFM Erwin Rommel commanded the actual fighting troops. Bastico had fallen out with Rommel over the strategy for retaking Tobruk in 1941 and remained hostile to the German commander for the rest of the campaign. In practice then, the Germans had taken over the running of the campaign and Rommel received his orders direct from the OKW in Berlin. The set-up was frustrating for Rommel, for most of the decisions regarding the crucial provision of supplies, shipping and transport were still controlled by the Italians and were not under his direct command. Throughout the campaign Rommel was to be plagued by these supply problems to such an extent that they had great influence on the outcome of several actions.

Generalfeldmarschall Erwin Rommel (1891–1944) had joined 6th Württemberg as an officer cadet in 1910. During the Great War he was in action in France, Romania and Italy. He was twice wounded and won the Iron Cross 1st and 2nd Class together with Germany's highest award for bravery, the *Pour le Mérite*. He later drew on his wartime experiences and wrote a book called *Infantry Tactics* which was met with great acclaim throughout Europe. Hitler was an admirer of the book and Rommel for a time commanded the Führer's security battalion. Rommel never qualified for the General Staff but still managed to achieve regular promotion during the inter-war period to reach the rank of Generalmajor in 1939. His actions in command of 7th Panzer Division in France in 1940 earned him a great reputation as an armoured commander. This reputation grew with successes in North Africa after he had taken over Axis armoured formations in March 1941. Nicknamed the 'Desert Fox', he quickly gained almost legendary status on both sides from his use of mobile forces. His superior tactical skill saw him achieve some remarkable victories, the most spectacular of which was at Gazala in May 1942.

The Desert Fox, Generalfeldmarschall Erwin Rommel, Commander *Panzerarmee Afrika*. Around his neck he wears the *Pour le Mérite* Cross that he won in the First War and the Knight's Cross of the Iron Cross with Oakleaves. He was awarded his Knight's Cross on 26 May 1940 and then became the tenth recipient of Oakleaves on 21 March 1941. Further awards followed; on 20 January 1942 he was the sixth person to be awarded Swords and on 11 March 1943 was the first non-Luftwaffe recipient of Diamonds to his Knight's Cross. (IWM GER 1281)

Three field marshals discuss the situation in Egypt. From left to right, GFM Erwin Rommel (Panzerarmee Afrika), GFM Albert Kesselring (German C-in-C Mediterranean) and Marshal Ugo Cavallero (Italian Commando Supremo). (Bundesarchiv 1011-786-0326-12)

Rommel visits the Afrika Korps' HQ in June 1942 to consult with some of its senior officers. From left to right, Oberst Fritz Bayerlein (Chief of Staff), Oberstleutnant Mellenthin (in charge of operations), GFM Rommel and GenLt Walther Nehring (Commander Afrika Korps). (Bundesarchiv 1011-784-0203-14A)

Rommel was made a field marshal by Hitler after his success in recapturing Tobruk in June 1942.

There were many other very able German commanders in North Africa, some of whom went on to greater things. **General der Panzertruppe Walther Nehring** led the Afrika Korps during First Alamein. He had served in the German infantry in the First World War and switched over to tanks in the 1930s. He commanded 18th Panzer Division in Russia before joining Rommel. By the end of the war he had risen to the command of First Panzer Army. After Nehring was wounded in the Alam Halfa battle, the Afrika Korps was commanded by **Generalleutnant Wilhelm Ritter von Thoma**. During the First World War he had fought with distinction and was awarded the Bavarian Order of Max-Josef and the title of Ritter. He was a professional soldier and pursued his career during the inter-war years in the Reichswehr and later in the Wehrmacht, becoming a specialist in the use of mobile forces. In Russia he had commanded both 6th and 20th Panzer Divisions.

Many of the Italian generals who commanded formations in Panzerarmee Afrika have come in for a good deal of criticism. They are often portrayed as being weak and ineffectual. This broad sweep of censure is often unfair. Although leadership at the top was consistently poor, some of the Italian divisions fought remarkably well in adversity and their generals did the best they could with the means available. **General Giuseppe de Stefanis**, commander of Italian XX Corps was a veteran leader of combat units in the First World War. He commanded the Pinerolo Division in Greece in 1941 and had won the *Ordine Militare di Savoia*, one of Italy's highest military awards. He had led both the Trento and Ariete Divisions in North Africa before being elevated to corps command.

OPPOSING ARMIES

T here is no doubt that at the end of June 1942, when Eighth Army had been forced back into Egypt and Rommel's army was in close pursuit, Auchinleck's forces were at a very low ebb. The strength that had been built up over the previous six months for the final offensive to push Rommel out of Africa had been squandered in a poorly fought battle at Gazala against an army commander who was a master of mobile tactics. The Gazala action and those skirmishes that followed did not, however, constitute a complete rout. Auchinleck had all the while kept his army in existence. Although much of his force was strung out across the desert and thoroughly disorganized, he still had confidence that he would be able to pull it together and face the enemy for what could be its final battle.

BRITISH FORCES

Early in 1942 Eighth Army had been forced to provide formations for the fighting in the Far East and it took time for new divisions and supplies to be shipped out from the UK to gradually build it back to full strength. Much of this new strength had been lost at Gazala, but Eight Army still remained a potent force when Rommel entered Egypt. The composition of Auchinleck's army during First Alamein was a mix of infantry and armoured formations from Britain and its Dominions. Many of these divisions, such as 7th Armoured Division (the Desert Rats), were veterans

British 6-pdr anti-tank gun in action. The arrival of the 6-pdr in North Africa in mid-1942 gave the British a powerful weapon with which to finally counter German tanks. Its 2.84kg shell could penetrate 50mm of armour at 1,500 metres. (IWM E15559)

of the fighting in North Africa with a long list of battle honours to their name. Others were newly arrived on the continent. There was a large contingent of divisions from the countries of the old British Empire, with formations arriving from New Zealand, Australia, South Africa and India. These were especially welcome for Britain struggling to raise enough equipped divisions for service on three continents, for these formations had a reputation for being aggressive in attack and dogged in defence. They were all well regarded by friend and foe alike.

In late June 1942, there were three corps in Eighth Army: X, XIII and XXX Corps. HQ X Corps, however, had arrived from Syria on 21 June, too late to have any part in stemming the German onslaught. During the first action at Alamein it remained in the delta. When Montgomery arrived in Egypt he decided to reconstitute this formation with armoured divisions as a

Early model American Stuart light tank in British service with riveted hull. The tank is from 7th Armoured Division and its crew are looking towards the high ground of Qaret el Himeimat. (IWM E16095)

mobile corps along the lines of the Afrika Korps. The other two corps fought in all three of the Alamein battles, with both armoured and infantry divisions under command.

Reinforcements for British units continued to arrive in North Africa in regular quantities which kept all formations up to near their nominal strength. Even so, there were times, especially after stiff actions, when numbers in the division fell to levels which required the unit to be pulled out of the line for rest and replenishment. Casualties were more of a problem for the Dominion divisions. Their replacements had to come from their own national reserves. This made losses in action keenly felt back home, which in turn created some disquiet among their politicians. Also bolstering British forces were contingents of troops from other European countries. The 1st Greek Brigade was used to hold

The first of the new Sherman tanks to arrive with Eighth Army were just in time to take part in the final battle of El Alamein. Until the German Tiger tank came onto the scene in Tunisia, the Sherman was able to engage all German armour in North Africa on more or less equal terms. (IWM E18380)

defensive positions in the line, and 1st and 2nd Free French Brigades were committed to secondary attacks on the edge of the Qattara Depression during the final battle at Alamein.

British and Commonwealth divisions were organized along similar lines. Infantry divisions contained three infantry brigades each with three rifle battalions, a reconnaissance regiment, a machine-gun battalion and three field and one anti-tank regiments of artillery. Armoured Divisions comprised one armoured and one motorized infantry brigade with two field and one anti-tank regiments of guns. Each armoured brigade contained three armoured regiments and one motor battalion. Up until First Alamein the artillery was distributed among brigades. Auchinleck changed this so that all of the guns were centralized under the command of Divisional HQ. This change was formalized for all divisions in August 1942.

While training and support for Eighth Army was quite adequate, weapons and equipment were often below the standards of the Germans. One of the great problems was in British tank design which, up until that time in the war, had not been very successful. They were often easily outperformed by German models. Crusader and Valentine tanks were the most numerous in the desert and both were armed with small 2-pdr (40mm) weapons, although some later-version Crusader IIIs with 6-pdr (57mm) guns were beginning to arrive in Egypt. The Crusader also had a reputation for being unreliable. Things improved somewhat with the arrival of the American-built Grant tank for this was armed with both a large 75mm gun and a 37mm weapon which could engage German tanks on something like an equal footing, but the tank had its disadvantages. Its main gun was sponson-mounted on its side and had a very limited traverse. Its three-metre high profile also towered over the battlefield making it very difficult for it to be concealed in the open desert. Just before Montgomery's final battle at El Alamein, American Sherman tanks began to arrive in the theatre. These had a turret-mounted 75mm gun, were capable of reasonably high speeds and were highly manoeuvrable. With them, the British finally had a tank that could match German armour.

German Luftwaffe SdKfz 7 medium tractor pulling an 88mm flak gun to be used in an anti-tank role. The gun already has a number of 'kills' to its credit as shown by the rings around its barrel near the muzzle. (IWM MH5833)

The other critical problem encountered by the British was the inadequacy of its main anti-tank gun, the 2-pdr (40mm). It just did not have enough punch to stop enemy tanks at anything like the distance they should be engaged. Fortunately, a new anti-tank gun, the 6-pdr (57mm), was beginning to arrive in Egypt in large numbers. This was a much more potent weapon and was quickly used to re-arm the anti-tank regiments of the Royal Artillery and then the anti-tank companies of the infantry battalions themselves. The sensible deployment of this type of gun curtailed Rommel's ability to charge at the British as he had done so often in the past.

One of the greatest advantages that Eighth Army had over the enemy was the support of Air Vice-Marshal Sir Arthur Coningham's Desert Air Force, flying from airstrips close to the action. During the earlier battles in Libya it was the German Luftwaffe and the Italian Regia Aeronautica that commanded the sky from their more local landing grounds. The further the Axis forces advanced into Egypt the less effective their air forces became. It was not just the long flying time to the front that put them at a disadvantage, the Desert Air Force had in the meantime gradually begun to obtain a numerical advantage over its rivals. By the time of the Alamein battles it had almost complete superiority over the enemy's air fleet and was able to bomb and strafe rear areas with such regularity that it had a marked effect on the conduct of the battles on the ground.

AXIS FORCES

Whilst Panzerarmee Afrika was not solely a German formation, its command was German, its strategy was German inspired and its tactical deployment was German led. Its main strike force was contained in the German Afrika Korps, with 15th and 21st Panzer Divisions. This crack formation was supported by the equally famous motorized 90th Light Division. A little later, in July 1942, these were joined by 164th Light 'Afrika' Division. All of these divisions were well trained, well led and highly mobile. They were the strike force of Rommel's army, but by no means his only mobile units.

Artillery crew of a German FH18 150mm field howitzer await orders to open fire. The gun could deliver a 43kg shell up to a distance of 13,325 metres. It became the standard German heavy field howitzer of the war. (Bundesarchiv 1011-783-0119-17A)

GFM Rommel inspects a knocked-out Stuart tank belonging to the headquarters of a British armoured battalion. (IWM MH5875)

An Italian M13/40 tank being unloaded from a transporter. The tank was slow, uncomfortable and under-powered, but still served as the basic armoured vehicle in all of the Italian armoured units. Its 47mm gun, however, was accurate and its armour-piercing capability was superior to the British Crusader and Valentine tanks which were armed with the 2-pdr gun. (Ufficio Storico Esercito Rome)

At First Alamein two Italian armoured divisions (Ariete and Littorio) and one motorized division (Trieste) were with Rommel, combined in Italian XX Corps. None of these divisions were quite as competent or as skilful as their German counterparts for they were let down by the ineffectiveness of their armour. They were, none the less, a vital link in Rommel's mobile tactics. The often maligned Italian infantry divisions with Panzerarmee Afrika were also indispensable. The Trento, Sabratha, Bologna, Brescia and Pavia Divisions grouped in X and XXI Corps were not as proficient as German formations, but could put up an effective fight when suitably led and deployed. They were used to hold the line, occupy territory and man fixed defences for just long enough to allow the armoured divisions to intervene. In some ways they were seen as 'cannon fodder', there to absorb the shock of any major attack. Such cynical use dispirited their commanders and affected morale in the ranks. Most Italian troops simply wished for a speedy end to the war so

Italian crew of a 149/40 Modello 35 gun. The 149 mm piece fired a 46 kg shell a maximum distance of 23,700 metres. Its large split trails used hammered spikes for anchoring. (Ufficio Storico Esercito Rome)

that they could all return home, their dreams of African conquests replaced by a determination to survive.

The Italian Army was inadequately served by its weapons. Its main tanks, the M13/40 and the M14/41 variant, were the poorest in Africa in terms of armament, armour protection and performance and its 47/32 M35 anti-tank gun had less penetrative power than the British 2-pdr gun. The same was not true of the equipment in the German arsenal, for it contained two very prominent weapons, the Panzer IV Special and the 88mm gun, that outperformed all else on the battlefield. The Panzer IV tank was the best of the German armour and it was further improved in the summer of 1942 by the introduction of a new longer-barrelled 75mm gun to become Panzer IVF2 with almost twice the penetrative power of its predecessor. It was true that not many of these tanks were available to Rommel during his initial move into Egypt, but when they did put in an appearance, they proved to be extremely effective. The 88mm gun was strictly speaking an anti-aircraft weapon, but when used in an anti-tank role it proved to be irresistible. The flat trajectory and high velocity of its shells outclassed every other weapon on the battlefield. Its one drawback was its high profile; it stood very tall in the open desert.

The two armoured divisions of the Afrika Korps both consisted of one Panzer and one Panzergrenadier regiments. The Italian armoured divisions were likewise configured with one tank regiment and one motorized infantry regiment. The German 90th and 164th Divisions had three motorized infantry regiments. Italian motorized and infantry divisions each contained just two regiments.

Rommel's problems were not confined to just countering the British, he also had to contend with the battle for supplies. The provision of vehicles, reinforcements, weapons and fuel were Panzerarmee Afrika's greatest worry. With the battered ports of Tripoli and Benghazi located hundreds of kilometres in the rear, the long trek to obtain sufficient quantities of supplies forwards into Egypt was a constant headache for Rommel. Everything required for battle had to be shipped across the Mediterranean Sea. There were often sufficient stores and transport available in Italy, but each ship bringing goods across to North Africa had to run the gauntlet of naval and air attacks from British forces based in Malta and Egypt. In July 1942 only 20 per cent of the required total was unloaded in Libya, whilst in August Rommel's army used up twice the amount that was landed. All stocks were running perilously low and the scarcity of fuel especially had a great influence on the shape of the battles fought in the summer of 1942.

ORDER OF BATTLE: BRITISH FORCES

Commander-in-Chief Middle East – Gen the Hon Sir Harold Alexander

British Eighth Army – LtGen Sir Bernard Montgomery

Army Troops
- 1st Anti-tank Brigade
- 1st Armoured Brigade
- 2nd Anti-aircraft Brigade
- 12th Anti-aircraft Brigade
- 21st Independent Infantry Brigade

X Corps – LtGen Herbert Lumsden

1st Armoured Division – MajGen R. Briggs
- 2nd Armoured Brigade
- 7th Motorized Brigade
- Hammerforce (From 8th Armoured Division)

8th Armoured Division – MajGen C.H. Gairdner
- 24th Armoured Brigade (To 10th Armoured Division)
- Hammerforce (To 1st Armoured Division)

10th Armoured Division – MajGen A.H. Gatehouse
- 8th Armoured Brigade
- 24th Armoured Brigade (From 8th Armoured Division)
- 133rd Lorried Infantry Brigade (From 44th Division)

XIII Corps – LtGen Brian Horrocks

7th Armoured Division – MajGen A.F. Harding
- 4th Light Armoured Brigade
- 22nd Armoured Brigade
- 1st Free French Brigade Group

44th Division – MajGen I.T.P. Hughes
- 131st Brigade
- 132nd Brigade
- 133rd Brigade (To 10th Armoured Division)

50th Division – MajGen J.S. Nichols
- 69th Infantry Brigade
- 151st Infantry Brigade
- 1st Greek Brigade
- 2nd Free French Brigade Group

XXX Corps – LtGen Sir Oliver Leese

23rd Armoured Brigade Group (Corps Reserve)

Indian 4th Division – MajGen F.I.S. Tuker
- 5th Indian Brigade
- 7th Indian Brigade
- 161st Indian Brigade

51st (Highland) Division – MajGen D.N. Wimberley
- 152nd Brigade
- 153rd Brigade
- 154th Brigade

Australian 9th Division – LtGen Sir Leslie Morshead
- 20th Australian Brigade
- 24th Australian Brigade
- 26th Australian Brigade

New Zealand 2nd Division – LtGen Sir Bernard Freyberg VC
- 5th New Zealand Brigade
- 6th New Zealand Brigade
- 9th Armoured Brigade

South African 1st Division MajGen D.H. Pienaar
- 1st South African Brigade
- 2nd South African Brigade
- 3rd South African Brigade

Troops of the South African 1st Division together with their Marmon Herrington armoured cars captured by Germans after the Gazala battles. (Bundesarchiv 1011-784-0232-22A)

German cans, called 'jerrycans' by the British, are being filled with water ready for transportation up to the forward positions. The prominent white crosses painted on the containers distinguish them from cans carrying petrol. (Bundesarchiv 1011-782-0033-16A)

Panzer IV with short-barrel 75mm gun from 8th Panzer Regiment of 15th Panzer Division. Its triangular divisional sign can be seen to the right of the driver's slit. (Bundesarchiv 1011-439-1276-12)

ORDER OF BATTLE: AXIS FORCES

Italian Commando Supremo – Benito Mussolini
    Chief of Staff – Marshal Count Ugo Cavallero

German Commander-in-Chief South – GFM Albert Kesselring

Italian Commando Supremo Africa – Marshal Ettore Bastico

Panzerarmee Afrika – GFM Erwin Rommel

ITALIAN FORCES

Italian X Corps – Gen Enrico Frattini (acting)

9th Regt Bersaglieri

17th Divisione di Fanteria 'Pavia' – Gen Nazareno Scattaglia
    27th Regt Fanteria
    28th Regt Fanteria

27th Divisione di Fanteria 'Brescia' – Gen Brunetto Brunetti
    19th Regt Fanteria
    20th Regt Fanteria

185th Divisione Paracadutisti 'Folgore' – Gen Enrico Frattini
    186th Regt Paracadutisti
    187th Regt Paracadutisti
    Raggruppamento 'Ruspoli' (Battle Group)

Italian XX Corps – Gen Giuseppe De Stefanis

101st Divisione Motorizzata 'Trieste' – Gen Francesco La Ferla
    65th Regt Fanteria Motorizzata
    66th Regt Fanteria Motorizzata
    VIII Battaglione Bersaglieri
    XI Battaglione Corazzato

132nd Divisione Corazzata 'Ariete' – Gen Francesco Arena
    132nd Regt Corazzato
    8th Regt Bersaglieri
    III Gruppo Squadroni 'Nizza Cavalleria'

133rd Divisione Corazzata 'Littorio' – Gen Gervasio Bitossi
    133rd Regt Corazzato
    12th Regt Bersaglieri
    III Gruppo Squadroni 'Lanceri de Novaria'

Italian XXI Corps – Gen Alessandro Gloria (acting)

7th Regt Bersaglieri

25th Divisione di Fanteria 'Bologna' – Gen Alessandro Gloria
    39th Regt Fanteria
    40th Regt Fanteria

102nd Divisione di Fanteria 'Trento' – Gen Giorgio Masina
    61st Regt Fanteria
    62nd Regt Fanteria

Italian Reserve (still forming)

136th Divisione Corazzata 'Giovani Fascisti' – Gen Ismaele di Nisio
    Regt Fanteria 'Giovani Fascisti'
    III Gruppo Squadroni 'Cavalleggeri di Monferrato'

GERMAN FORCES

90th Leichte Division – GenLt Theodor Graf von Sponeck
    155th Regiment
    200th Regiment
    361st Motorized Regiment

164th Leichte 'Afrika' Division – GenMaj Carl-Hans Lungershausen
    125th Panzergrenadier Regiment
    382nd Panzergrenadier Regiment
    433rd Panzergrenadier Regiment

Ramcke Parachute Brigade – GenMaj Hermann-Bernhard Ramcke

Deutsches Afrika Korps – GenLt Wilhelm Ritter von Thoma

15th Panzer Division – GenMaj Gustav von Vaerst
    8th Panzer Regiment
    115th Panzergrenadier Regiment

21st Panzer Division – GenMaj Heinz von Randow
    5th Panzer Regiment
    104th Panzergrenadier Regiment

OPPOSING PLANS

At the end of June 1942, when Gen Auchinleck's forces had been forced right back inside Egypt after suffering great losses in men and *matériel*, defeat was a distinct possibility. In contrast, Rommel's Panzerarmee Afrika was brimful of confidence after weeks of success, it had the smell of victory in its nostrils and was on the point of driving the British out of Egypt. At least, that is how it appeared to those who were there and to governments overseas. This appreciation was, however, flawed. The British had actually fallen back into a defendable position and could call on fresh troops previously withdrawn from the action. Other divisions were also at that moment en route for Egypt. Their lines of communication had shortened and reinforcements, tanks, fuel and new equipment were still arriving in the ports just 120 kilometres to their rear. In contrast, Rommel's forces were all exhausted. Their petrol supplies had almost dried up; their tank numbers had dwindled through breakdowns and losses; supply lines snaked back for hundreds of kilometres across the desert to bomb-damaged ports in their rear and they were short of reinforcements, fuel, tanks, transport and guns. On paper at least, it looked as though Rommel could not go on. His superiors, Kesselring, Cavallero and Bastico, all agreed that he had overextended himself; all originally urged him to stop. He would have none of it; the Nile Delta seemed there for the taking.

The British had been brought to this unenviable position by a tactically superior enemy. Rommel's reputation rested on his use of his mobile forces. When he arrived just short of Alamein on 29 June he believed he had the British on the run. It was therefore essential that he kept up the momentum; to delay would be fatal. He knew that he would have to force the Alamein line and relied on his momentum to take him through. He could not afford to wait for his exhausted force to gather strength and let his supply lines catch up with him, for the British would also use the time to rest and improve their defences. Rommel saw the Alamein position as another line on which to employ his usual tactics of a frontal assault by infantry and a wide sweep by the Afrika Korps to move behind the defenders, a plan that had worked so well in the past.

Auchinleck also stuck to the strategy he had used before. He would fight Rommel on this new defence line and, whatever happened, he would keep Eighth Army intact. If he was forced into another retreat then he would pull back to the next position already hurriedly being prepared in front of the delta in his rear. In the meantime he would fight a battle at Alamein. Tactically he would use the same plan as Rommel but in reverse. He could not man the whole of the line, so he would put strong positions of infantry and guns in 'boxes' in and around selected features, blocking the route, and then attack any penetrations between them with mobile groups. As Rommel manoeuvred to find an

Group of German officers from the Afrika Korps waiting for the start of an attack. (Bundesarchiv 1011-782-0023-09A)

opening, Auchinleck would manoeuvre to prevent it. It was a good plan, for it worked.

Rommel's dash for the delta was halted in a battle that was to become known as First Alamein. Auchinleck then proceeded to construct a thick line of defences to deal with the next Axis attack, paying special attention to the northern sector which he had extensively mined in an effort to force Rommel to consider attacking in the south, past the long Alam Halfa Ridge. Auchinleck rightly determined that this ridge would be the key to the next battle, for Rommel would have to either pass alongside it or manoeuvre round it. Either way, Auchinleck intended to be ready for him. Then things changed; Churchill urged Auchinleck to go back on the offensive while Rommel gathered strength for his next push for the Suez Canal, but Auchinleck insisted on more time. Churchill would not agree on any further

A near miss as a mine explodes close by some British transport, although this is probably a staged incident laid on for the photographers. (IWM E18542)

delay and Auchinleck was replaced by LtGen Bernard Montgomery. Exasperatingly for Churchill, Montgomery also decided he would not go over to the offensive straight away. He would wait until he had seen off Rommel's next attempt at a breakthrough. Once Rommel had been halted, he would put in his attack, but even then he would not make his move until he had overwhelming superiority in men and weapons, and not before Eighth Army had reached a standard of training that met with his own high ideals.

Auchinleck had evolved certain tactics for defensive action in the desert. He realized that the wide featureless terrain made static positions alone ineffective – they could be easily outflanked. It was important to be able to move and concentrate against the point of enemy penetration and to bring upon him the greatest amount of firepower that was available. It was also pointless to have too many infantry in defensive positions, but those that were there needed to have sufficient anti-tank and artillery to provide an all-round defence. There also had to be an overall balance between those troops and artillery holding the line and those that were committed to a mobile role. Units and headquarters in the immediate rear had to be prepared to defend themselves in the event that the enemy managed to break through the forward positions and overrun them. They also had to be able to hold out until mobile forces were able to help clear away the enemy. This doctrine led to the arrangement of defence localities termed 'boxes', which usually contained two battalions of infantry, and a battery each of field, anti-aircraft and anti-tank guns. The remainder of the division was organized into mobile groups.

German soldier attempting to dig a 'foxhole' in the stony desert. With little natural cover, it was important to get below ground as soon as possible for safety. (IWM MH5834)

Montgomery did not like the idea of boxes. He thought that divisions should fight as divisions with all their artillery massed in support. He also took note from Rommel and created a mobile corps of his own, modelled along similar lines to the Afrika Korps, to be held in reserve and used as a strike force. He planned to continue Auchinleck's work to heavily fortify the northern sector of the line to a point where Rommel could only realistically make his attack in the south. Montgomery would

German signals post near Tel el Eisa. The flat featureless terrain made it possible to transmit (and listen to) radio traffic over large distances. The Germans gained much important intelligence by listening to the insecure chatter of British units talking to each other in plain language. (IWM MH 5581)

then mass his guns and assemble his armour to meet him, just as Auchinleck had intended.

It has to be noted that both Montgomery and Auchinleck were helped in making this decision by the use of ULTRA intercepts. The breaking of the German codes allowed both of these commanders to have an insight into Axis thinking. Such gathering of intelligence was not, however, all one-sided for the Germans were also receiving a wealth of information about British forces from two individual sources. The most important was from their own specialist listening service located in the desert, which was picking up and analysing insecure radio chatter emanating from Eighth Army. It was amazing just what could be deduced from units talking to each other over the air. More valuable news, possibly much more valuable at a higher level, was obtained by deciphering dispatches sent to Washington by Col Bonner Fellers, the US military attaché in Cairo. The Italians and Germans were both able to decipher American codes from the 'Black Book' encryption that Fellers used. The nightly dispatches radioed to the USA after he had visited British formations and talked with senior commanders was decoded by the enemy before morning. When America entered the war Fellers had privileged access to the most sensitive of information and all of this fell into German hands. The Germans later admitted that the information unwittingly supplied by Fellers contributed decisively to their victories in North Africa.

Rommel's last attack was emphatically turned back in the battle of Alam Halfa and hopes for a renewed push to the delta faded forever. Rommel knew that it was now the turn of the British to make their attack. All he could do was strengthen his defences and make ready to deal with the onslaught when it came. His plan rested on having defences of such thickness and depth that they were capable of holding the enemy back. In the event of a British penetration, his mobile armoured forces would then advance to seal it off. To counter this, Montgomery could only use brute force and overwhelming numbers. He knew that he would have to attack very strong positions and would take large numbers of casualties. The battle of attrition which would follow would have to be endured long enough for gaps to be opened for the tanks to pass through and be ready to meet with the Axis armour which would inevitably come at them. Then it would be down to a dog fight to see who was the strongest.

FIRST ALAMEIN

The El Alamein line into which Eighth Army retreated in late June was a defence line in name only. Very little had been done to prepare the ground in terms of field fortifications; its main strength was its natural location. The line stretched north to south across 65 kilometres of desert over several low ridges and shallow depressions. Anchoring the northern flank was the sea. In the south was the Qattara Depression, a massive area of soft sand and salt marsh, impassable to tanks and most kinds of transport. The Alamein line could not therefore be outflanked; Rommel would have to come through it. Attempting to block his way were three defended localities about 25 kilometres apart, the first around the railway station at El Alamein, the second in the middle of the line about Bab el Qattara and the third close to the great depression at Naqb Abu. None of these localities had been properly wired or mined.

The original German plan was for Axis forces to pause for six weeks for resupply after the capture of Tobruk, but the collapse of the British forces after Gazala led to approval being given to Rommel to advance straight into Egypt. On 28 June, after some initial reluctance on the part of senior commanders in the Mediterranean, he received specific orders to defeat the forces opposing him, seize the Suez Canal between Ismailia and Port Said, occupy Cairo and eradicate any possible threat from Alexandria. Cairo lay just 160 kilometres away and Rommel knew that if he paused he would be giving Auchinleck time to reorganize. Delay

The isolated railway station of El Alamein gave its name to the famous battle which was fought in the desert to the south. In 1942 there were just a few buildings clustered round the station, tens of miles from any other habitation. (IWM E14398)

FIRST ALAMEIN

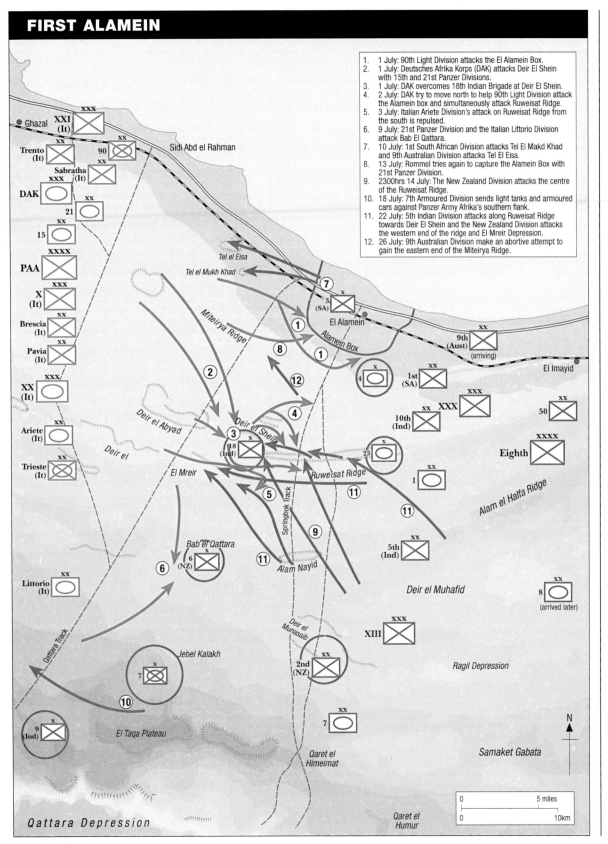

1. 1 July: 90th Light Division attacks the El Alamein Box.
2. 1 July: Deutsches Afrika Korps (DAK) attacks Deir El Shein with 15th and 21st Panzer Divisions.
3. 1 July: DAK overcomes 18th Indian Brigade at Deir El Shein.
4. 2 July: DAK try to move north to help 90th Light Division attack the Alamein box and simultaneously attack Ruweisat Ridge.
5. 3 July: Italian Ariete Division's attack on Ruweisat Ridge from the south is repulsed.
6. 9 July: 21st Panzer Division and the Italian Littorio Division attack Bab El Qattara.
7. 10 July: 1st South African Division attacks Tel El Makd Khad and 9th Australian Division attacks Tel El Eisa.
8. 13 July: Rommel tries again to capture the Alamein Box with 21st Panzer Division.
9. 2300hrs 14 July: The New Zealand Division attacks the centre of the Ruweisat Ridge.
10. 18 July: 7th Armoured Division sends light tanks and armoured cars against Panzer Army Afrika's southern flank.
11. 22 July: 5th Indian Division attacks along Ruweisat Ridge towards Deir El Shein and the New Zealand Division attacks the western end of the ridge and El Mreir Depression.
12. 26 July: 9th Australian Division make an abortive attempt to gain the eastern end of the Miteirya Ridge.

33

These motorcyclists are totally exhausted and have fallen asleep where they stopped. The 'WL' number plate shows them to be Luftwaffe troops, probably attached to one of the flak batteries. The Afrika Korps palm tree and Swastika insignia can be seen on the front of the sidecar. (Bundesarchiv 1011-782-0041-32)

would be fatal. He realized that he would have to force the Alamein line without halting, even though his men were tired, his equipment was in need of repair and his supply lines stretched almost to breaking point. On 29 June, immediately after 90th Light Division had captured the Mursa Matruh position, Rommel sent the division eastwards with the armour of the Afrika Korps to make renewed contact with Eighth Army, their transport refuelled from stocks captured from the British.

In Alexandria and Cairo confusion reigned. Sympathetic Arabs began to prepare for the arrival of Rommel, openly sneering at the plight of the British. Panic set in amongst the rear areas; confidential documents were burned; elements of the Middle East Headquarters were moved to Palestine; the Mediterranean Fleet left Alexandria to disperse amongst the safer ports of Haifa and Beirut and arrangements were made to block the harbour and destroy port facilities and stores.

On 30 June Rommel had his strike force ready to attack between the Alamein position and Deir el Abyad. The 90th Light Division was on the left and his two panzer divisions abreast of it on the right. He intended to pass the armour down the southern side of the Miteirya Ridge towards the British near Ruweisat Ridge. The 90th would skirt the Alamein defences and then cut them off from the east while the Afrika Korps was swinging south to Alam Nayil to take British XIII Corps in the rear. Italian XXI Corps would come forward next and attack Alamein directly from the west. Italian XX Corps was to follow behind the panzer divisions then swing south to attack the Bab el Qattara position.

In the early hours of 1 July, 90th Light Division attacked eastwards intending to pass to the south of the El Alamein Box. In poor light and a sandstorm the leading units quickly lost their way and collided with the Alamein defences. The exhausted Panzergrenadiers soon became entangled in vicious fighting by an enemy who was better prepared than they expected him to be. It was not until early afternoon that the division was able to resume its advance. To the south the Afrika Korps fared little better. Both 15th and 21st Panzer Divisions found their approach to the start line difficult and arrived three hours late, bombed and disorganized by the Desert Air Force. When the advance finally got

The lonely figure of Gen Claude Auchinleck watches the last of his units arrive into the Alamein line after the rout suffered at Gazala and Mersa Matruh at the end of June 1942. (IWM E13882)

under way, they found that the area around Deir el Shein before the Ruweisat Ridge was held in some strength by 18th Indian Brigade. The brigade was newly arrived from Iraq and had been placed under the command of South African 1st Division. The panzers now came under heavy artillery fire from the Indians and the South African Division. This was something of a shock for Gen d.Pz Walther Nehring, commander of the Afrika Korps, for intelligence had suggested that these troops were much further to the east. Nehring felt that he had no option but to attack the position. This was no easy task and it was not until 1900hrs that evening that his panzer divisions managed to overwhelm the stiff resistance put up by 18th Indian Brigade and take Deir el Shein, losing 18 of its precious 55 tanks in the process.

Meanwhile, 90th Light Division had also had a bad afternoon. On its attempt to get around to the east of the Alamein Box it had run into terrific artillery fire from the guns of the South African Division and had gone to ground. Rommel's personal intervention was unable to get it moving again, for the army commander himself was caught in the barrage and forced to lay on the open ground with his troops for three hours. Further back, the Italians were attacking the other end of the Alamein position with little success.

While Rommel was face-down in the sand, Auchinleck was issuing orders for a counterattack. It had been a good day for Eighth Army's commander. His forces, suitably supported by the Desert Air Force, had blunted Rommel's first attempt to get past the Alamein line. He had lost the 18th Indian Brigade but had halted the Afrika Korps, and the slow collapse of the position at Deir el Shein through the resistance put up by the Indians had allowed Auchinleck to gather fresh forces to block the Germans. It was now essential that his defence should include tactical attacks to deflect Rommel's intentions.

Auchinleck ordered LtGen Norrie's XXX Corps to hold Rommel's advance while LtGen Gott's XIII Corps hit his right flank with armour. Gott was told to attack on either side of the Ruweisat Ridge towards Deir el Abyad. Now with both 90th Light Division and the Afrika Korps identified in the north, Auchinleck also decided that the defended localities of Bab el Qattara and Naqb abu Dweis could be abandoned to make his defence more compact. The New Zealand Division could be withdrawn and prepared for a mobile role, as could Indian 5th Division in the south.

The next day, 2 July, the German 90th Division failed to get moving again in the face of heavy British artillery fire. Rommel realized that he would have to shift some of his weight to the north to help the division to get eastwards along the coast road. Nehring's corps was ordered to detach some of his tanks break to give some support to the 90th Light Division.

The renewed German thrust and the British counter attack got underway simultaneously. The clash rippled across the northern part of the Alamein line. Fierce fighting, both north and south of the Ruweisat Ridge and on the ridge itself lasted until dark. Tanks of the 1st

TANKS AND ANTI-TANK GUNS OF THE ITALIAN ARIETE DIVISION ATTACKING SOUTH OF RUWEISAT RIDGE DURING THE FIRST BATTLE OF EL ALAMEIN (pages 36–37)

The main German effort on 3 July lay south of the Ruweisat Ridge. The Afrika Korps launched an advance but soon ran into British armour, readying themselves for their own attack. The action was short and sharp, during which the Afrika Korps was firmly held by 1st Armoured Division. A little further to the south, British XIII Corps was also beginning an advance, aiming for Deir el Shein. It soon clashed with the Italian Ariete Division, which was putting in its own attack to the right of the Afrika Korps. The Italians were met with a fierce exchange of artillery which was followed up by the infantry of the New Zealand Division. Over 350 Italians were taken prisoner and 44 guns were captured. The New Zealanders then manoeuvred to try cut off the retreat of the Ariete, but found themselves engaged by the Brescia Division of Italian X Corps in the depression of El Mreir and had to retire. The battlescene shows M13/40 tanks of 1st Battalion of the Italian 132nd Ariete Armoured Division advancing eastwards during the attack. The division had performed well in the earlier Gazala and 'Knightsbridge' battles and Rommel thought it was one of the better Italian formations. The M13/40 tank (1) was the least effective fighting vehicle in the desert, generally inferior to all other

tanks, but available to the Italians in relatively large numbers - almost 2,000 were built during the war. It had a slow cross-country performance, only able to reach speeds of around 15 km/hour in action. It did, however, have an accurate 47mm gun with an armour-piercing capability superior to the under-gunned British tanks of the period before Alamein. It was effective against infantry, but unable to perform well against the faster and more heavily armoured tanks of Eighth Army. The tank had a crew of four, consisting of commander, loader, driver and radio operator/machine-gunner. It did not have a specific gunner, so the commander (2) also had to operate the main gun in addition to his other duties. The Italian 47mm anti-tank gun (3) was a useful weapon in the desert. Based on the Austrian 4.7mm Böhler anti-tank gun, it did not have the range of the devastating dual-purpose German 88mm gun, but it had a much lower profile, was easier to dig in and was often only detectable by British tank crews when it was too late to avoid its fire. The gun did not have a shield for protection, which exposed its crew to the effects of high-explosive shell fire. Supporting the advance is a self-propelled Semovente M40 75/18 assault gun (4). It consisted of a large 75mm gun mounted on an M40 chassis and gave the Italians unequalled fire power on the desert floor, but its low speed and thin armour made it vulnerable to British tanks and artillery. (Howard Gerrard)

Armoured Division were held by the anti-tank guns of the panzer divisions and Nehring's armour was corralled on the northern side of the ridge by the British artillery. The result was indecisive: Rommel's tired forces were too weak to push aside Auchinleck's troops and the British were too disorganized to completely repulse the advance. Eleven more German tanks had been lost in the action, reducing the DAK's panzer force to just 26 runners.

That night, his sleep broken by British bombing raids, Rommel decided to try again the next day to effect a breakthrough. He intended to probe the British defences to find a weak spot. The DAK was to renew its eastwards thrust while the Italian XX Corps advanced on its right flank; Italian X Corps was to hold El Mreir. Rommel knew that his men were exhausted, but reasoned that the British were also close to collapse; one big push would break the line. Auchinleck, in turn, still favoured an active defence and ordered XIII Corps to advance north-west of Deir el Shein in order to threaten the enemy's rear.

The main German effort on 3 July lay south of the Ruweisat Ridge. Early that morning the advance by the Afrika Korps ran into the British armour readying themselves for their attack. The action lasted for over an hour-and-a-half by which time the Germans had virtually reached the limit of their endurance. Rommel continued to urge his men on, but little further progress was made. The Afrika Korps was firmly held by 1st Armoured Division. Just to the south, British XIII Corps was beginning its advance on Deir el Shein when it bumped into the flanks of Italian Ariete Division who were crossing its front. An exchange of artillery was followed up by an attack by the New Zealand Division in which 350 prisoners and 44 guns were taken. The New Zealanders then manoeuvred to try to cut off the retreat of the Ariete, but found themselves engaged by the Brescia Division of Italian X Corps in the depression of El Mreir. The third day of the battle closed with little further progress by either side having been made, but it was the British who could most feel pleased with themselves. The Axis advance to the Nile Delta had been stopped in the north, in the centre and in the south on the scratch defence line of El Alamein.

Rommel now realized that he and his troops had reached their limit; they were all exhausted. He had to accept that his quick dash for Cairo was over. He gave orders for the Afrika Korps to pull back from the line the next day and hand over their positions to Italian infantry. The field marshal had not given up on his goal of seizing the Suez Canal, he was just taking stock before he launched a renewed attempt. In the meantime, he ordered minefields to be laid and defensive positions to be dug. Auchinleck at the same time was trying to figure out his next move. He had stopped Rommel's attack and now outlined his future intentions to his corps commanders, Norrie and Gott. The Axis forces must be completely destroyed, he explained, and he would do this by containing the enemy's eastern and southern flanks then attacking his rear. The whole of XIII Corps, together with 7th Motor and 4th Armoured Brigades would drive into Rommel's right rear and then roll up Panzerarmee Afrika from the south. 'The enemy must be given no rest,' he ordered.

On 4 July the British moves began, but found that the German withdrawals they detected the night before had not taken place. Immediately the armoured brigades advanced they met an enemy anti-tank screen and were stopped. A little to the south the New Zealand Division applied pressure against an ineffectual Italian opposition at El Mreir and 1st Armoured Division probed gingerly in the north. All of these moves were half-hearted attempts, although they did clear the enemy off a great part of the Ruweisat Ridge. As the official history of the campaign commented: 'The 4th July was a day of disjointed engagements which had no significant results.' The troops of Eighth Army and their commanders were all tired; no great effort was forthcoming.

The next day Auchinleck tried to reposition his forces to continue with the left hook that he had planned, but eventually realized that with his limited amount of armour it might be more prudent to try a more shallow hook aimed at Deir el Shein. Both corps were now ordered to concentrate their efforts towards this depression to the south west of the

British patrol behind enemy lines intercept an Axis truck and capture the occupants. The event is re-staged for the benefit of an accompanying photographer (IWM E12810)

Ruweisat Ridge. This they did over the next few days, but again the results were disappointing, with little new ground taken. At the same time, Rommel reasoned that as Auchinleck was shifting more and more of his strength in the north, he might try a move in the south aimed at first taking Bab el Qattara, then sweeping northwards to get behind British XIII Corps. The attack was planned for 9 July.

Auchinleck was pre-warned of these moves by ULTRA intercepts and decided that he would also attack, this time in the far north from out of the Alamein Box. He ordered LtGen W.H. Ramsden, the new commander of XXX Corps, to capture Tel el Eisa and Tel el Makh Khad. Both were defended by Italians and air reconnaissance showed that their defences were not highly developed. The capture of these two features would put a salient into Rommel's positions from which mobile forces could move towards the Miteirya Ridge and Deir el Shein.

The move would also threaten the enemy's supply line along the coastal road. Gott's XIII Corps was to prevent the enemy reinforcing the coastal sector during the attack. Ramsden had the use of both the South African Division and the newly arrived Australian 9th Division for the operation. The attack was planned for 10 July.

On 9 July Rommel attacked the now abandoned Bab el Qattara defensive position. A set-piece assault was put in by 21st Panzer and the Littorio Armoured Division. Not surprisingly the move was completely successful. Rommel thought that he had found a weak spot and ordered his troops to thrust southwards to Qaret el Himeimat, also calling the 90th Light Division forwards to push eastwards to find a way around the Eighth Army's southern flank. As they did so, in the early hours of 10 July, a threatening rumble of guns was heard from the north. Auchinleck's forces were also on the move.

Australian 9th Division and South African 1st Division, backed by armour, attacked out of the Alamein Box behind a very strong artillery barrage of an intensity not yet seen in the desert. The Italians were taken completely by surprise and lost virtually the whole of the Sabratha Division and a large part of the Trieste. By 1000hrs the South Africans were on Tel el Makd Khad and the Australians had cleared the coastal side of the railway and were attacking Tel el Eisa, overrunning the important German radio intercept unit that had given Rommel so much information on British movements over the previous year.

On hearing news of the British attack, Rommel left Bab el Qattara and sped north, collecting a battle group of 15th Panzer Division on the way. He feared disaster, later admitting that he thought the enemy was in hot pursuit westwards scattering the fleeing Italians and destroying his supplies. The German 164th Division was at that time in the process of arriving on the front and its 382nd Regiment was immediately sent to engage the Australians. This counterattack was held by LtGen Morshead's division and the next day it succeeded in capturing the whole of Tel el Eisa. Over the next four days Rommel's forces tried again and again to evict the Australians from this feature covering the western approach to Alamein, but the Commonwealth troops held on to their gains. Unfortunately the South Africans had withdrawn from Tel el Makh Khad through some misunderstanding of their orders. Rommel had prevented a catastrophe, but at the expense of using the troops he was gathering for his own renewed advance. He now admitted that British Eighth Army was in the hands of a new commander who was deploying his forces 'with considerable skill.' Rommel was finally being forced to dance to someone else's tune.

On 12 and 13 July the enemy continued to attack the Tel el Eisa salient. Rommel also tried to cut it off by attacking the Alamein Box, but both efforts failed. On the night of 14 July Auchinleck launched a new attack along the line of the Ruweisat Ridge aiming to break through the enemy's centre. XXX and XIII Corps assaulted the ridge together. On the right, Indian 5th Division (XXX Corps) attacked Point 64 on the centre of the feature, the New Zealand Division (XIII Corps) was on the left attacking Point 63 at the western end of the ridge and the 1st Armoured Division gave support along the line of the inter-corps boundary. The night attack was preceded by Albacore aircraft dropping flares and fighter-bombers strafing the enemy lines.

At first both divisions made good progress as they fought their way through the Italian Brescia and Pavia Divisions who were holding the ridge. The advance slowed down when they met extensive minefields and there was some loss of cohesion when the New Zealanders were attacked by tanks from 8th Panzer Regiment of 15th Panzer Division and lost 350 prisoners. Throughout the day the pressure applied by the British forced the two Italian divisions to give way and by late afternoon of 15 July both Points 63 and 64 were taken and most of the ridge was in Eighth Army's hands. The 1st Armoured Division remained further back ready to exploit a breakthrough.

Rommel originally thought that the attack was just a large raid against the Ruweisat Ridge, believing that Auchinleck would continue with his main effort nearer the coast, but when news of the collapse of the Pavia and Brescia Divisions reached him he realized that something much bigger was afoot. He immediately ordered German troops to the spot. To lead the counterattack against Ruweisat Ridge Rommel used the reconnaissance units of his panzer divisions and these hit the New Zealanders with some force, pushing them off the western end of the feature. The ferocity of the attack carried the Panzer reconnaissance troops down the slopes, overrunning the HQ of 4th New Zealand

Brigade and capturing the whole of the HQ staff, including Brigadier Burrows. The British armour meanwhile continued to stand back and wait for the right moment to counter attack. The right moment never came, for the New Zealanders continued to be pushed back and the German advance only came to a halt when it brushed up against 1st Armoured Division itself. The day had been saved once again for the Axis army by Rommel's speedy deployment of scratch units and once again the field marshal had been given a nasty scare.

Auchinleck's attack had gained half of the Ruweisat Ridge, but had fallen well short of his original intentions. The early successes of the Indian and the New Zealand Divisions had not been exploited by the tanks and there remained a great antipathy between the armour and the infantry commanders. The Commonwealth troops in particular had a very poor opinion of the effectiveness of British tank support. Infantry/armour co-operation was at an all-time low.

During the night of 15 July Rommel remained concerned that the British would attack again with armour. To forestall this, the next day he ordered an assault to be made on the Indian 5th Division near Point 64. In the event this came to nothing. The Australians also attacked out of their salient at Tel el Eisa towards the Miteirya Ridge, but they, too, made little progress. The next day it was more of the same, both sides made attempts to take new ground only to be turned back by solid defences. One item of significance did take place, however, when the Desert Air Force managed to fly 641 sorties, a record number for a single day. At the end of Auchinleck's attacks all that had substantially changed was that the British held the eastern half of Ruweisat and were faced by Germans instead of Italians. None the less, much had still been achieved in that Rommel now abandoned any thought of further attacks. His situation had been made worse by the loss of 2,200 tons of ammunition and 50,000 gallons of fuel to the bombs of the Desert Air Force during raids on Matruh.

On 18 July, 7th Armoured Division sent light tanks and armoured cars out into the desert in the extreme south of the line to harass and confuse the flank of Panzerarmee Afrika.

These moves acted as a diversion, for Auchinleck was on the offensive again, trying to engineer the breakthrough that he still thought was within his grasp. Spurred on by the endless urgings of Churchill, Eighth Army's commander launched another assault. On 22 July, 5th Indian Division attacked along Ruweisat Ridge towards Deir El Shein and the New Zealand Division attacked the western end of the ridge and El Mreir Depression. Opposing them were the Italian Brescia Division in Deir el Shein and the 21st Panzer Division on the western end of the ridge. Both Commonwealth Divisions made it to their objectives, but both were evicted by the 5th and 8th Panzer Regiments before British armoured support could get up to them. When the British tanks did eventually make contact with the Germans they suffered tremendous casualties, losing 132 of their number during the day against the loss of just three of the enemy. Indian 5th Division tried again along the ridge on 23 July, but its efforts ended in failure.

Despite every attack failing to crack the enemy's defences, Auchinleck had still not given up on his desire of breaking through Rommel's line. Once again he switched his effort to the coastal sector and on 26 July, Australian 9th Division and South African 1st Division made an attempt to gain the eastern end of the Miteirya Ridge. Gaps were made in Axis minefields and infantry went through, but all efforts were repulsed before armoured support could get forward to help. The fighting spilled into the next day but the moment was lost and the abortive attack was called off.

Auchinleck now followed Rommel's earlier decision and also went on to the defensive. He issued instruction to his corps commanders to strengthen their defences, rehearse plans for meeting any enemy attack and to rest, reorganize and re-train their troops. Auchinleck was sure that Rommel would not resume his attacks before he had likewise rested and gained strength. The first battle of Alamein was over. Rommel had been stopped and the initiative had been wrested from him. Eighth Army was beginning to believe that Rommel could eventually be beaten, but there was still a long way to go and a lot of hard fighting to be done.

BATTLE OF ALAM HALFA

A uchinleck had stopped Panerarmee Afrika, but the danger had not gone away. Rommel's forces were still gathered within Egypt and were gaining strength for a new push into the Delta. In the north, Gen Navarini's Italian XXI Corps held the line, with German 164th Division superimposed on the Trento and Bologna Divisions between the sea and Deir el Shein. The southern sector was the responsibility of Italian X Corps, commanded by Gen Orsi, with the Brescia Division and GenMaj Ramcke's 288th Parachute Brigade holding from Deir el Shein to Gebel Kalakh. The Folgore Parachute Division guarded the remainder of the line southwards to Naqb abu Dweis. In reserve were the two mobile corps, with de Stefanis' XX corps containing the Ariete and Littorio Armoured Divisions and the Trieste Motorized Division, lined up in positions behind the infantry. Nehring's Afrika Korps with the 15th and 21st Panzer Divisions was in army reserve. The 90th Light Division was out of the line resting.

Facing the enemy, Eighth Army began to lay extensive minefields and organize defensive positions ready to receive Rommel's forces should they decide to continue the attack. The northern sector near the coast was held by Australian 9th Division of XXX Corps. Then came South African 1st Division and Indian 5th Division holding the line down to the Ruweisat Ridge. In reserve behind them was 23rd Armoured Brigade. South of the ridge was XIII Corps. The New Zealand 2nd Division and 7th Armoured Division held the line southwards to Himeimat. The 1st Armoured Division was the mobile reserve.

First Alamein was initially seen as a great victory, but this feeling soon turned into the depressing realization that Eight Army had achieved little in the long term. After over two years of fighting, the British were back where they started from. This state of affairs drew great criticism from those responsible for the direction of the war in London. Auchinleck further annoyed Churchill when he declared that he could not resume the attack against Rommel until at least the middle of September. He army was tired and needed reinforcement, resupply and retraining. Churchill, ever the belligerent, was beginning to lose patience. He conferred with his Cabinet and with his Chief of the Imperial General Staff, Gen Sir Alan Brooke, and decided that changes would be made.

There was much political manoeuvring about how these changes would be resolved, with Churchill and Brooke arguing as to who would be best for each job. A compromise was reached in August when they both visited Egypt, whereby Auchinleck was relieved of his command and replaced by Gen Sir Harold Alexander as C-in-C Middle East and LtGen Sir Bernard Montgomery was designated Commander Eighth Army. Montgomery was not Churchill's first choice, although he was

German Panzergrenadier lifting a British anti-tank mine prior to the Alam Halfa battle. (IWM MH 5863)

Brooke's. Churchill had originally insisted that there should be some continuity of command in the desert rather than a wholesale replacement of leaders from outside the theatre. He demanded that LtGen Gott should move from XXX Corps to take over Eighth Army, even though the corps commander was exhausted by his long stay in the desert and needed a rest. Churchill, as usual, got his own way and Gott was appointed to the command. Fate, however, intervened when Gott was killed a few days later in an air crash.

The appointment of Montgomery to the command of Eighth Army has been seen as one of the greatest strokes of good fortune of the war for the British Army. Virtually unknown outside the military when he arrived, Montgomery soon became Britain's greatest commander of the war. Great in terms of his successes and fame, but perhaps not so great in his pursuit of self-aggrandizement and in his relationships with others. For every admirer to which he could do no wrong, there was a detractor full of criticism regarding his conduct. But there is no doubt that his arrival in Eighth Army was a breath of fresh air. From the very moment he arrived he began moulding his new army into a formation that met with his rigid approval. After a two-year seesaw of victories and defeats, Montgomery was determined to 'kick Rommel out of Africa for good'.

LtGen Montgomery instigated many changes in his command. He urged much closer co-operation between ground forces and the Desert Air Force. He insisted that his divisions would fight as divisions together with all their supporting arms, there would be no more fragmentation of effort. He was adamant that he would not attack until his numerical strength was much greater than the enemy, and that all of his men were properly trained and equipped for the tasks they would be given in battle. He maintained that all of his orders would be meticulously carried out and that there would be no 'bellyaching'. At Alamein, as in all of his future battles, he would not move until he was ready and only then with overwhelming force. There was a new commander at the head of Eighth Army, and everyone knew it.

To command XIII Corps in place of Gott, Montgomery brought out LtGen Brian Horrocks from England. The forty-six-year-old Horrocks had worked with Monty in South Eastern Command and had impressed his boss with his energetic enthusiasm. He had seen action as a battalion commander in France in 1940 before taking over a brigade and then helped train both 44th and 9th Armoured Divisions as their GOC.

July and August were spent by both sides building up their forces ready to launch an attack. Just prior to the renewal of the advance eastwards the main tank strength of Panzerarmee Afrika was 443, comprising 200 German and 243 Italian tanks. Of these, twenty-six were the new Panzer IV Specials with the long 75mm gun, ten were older Panzer IVs with the short-barrel gun, 71 were Panzer IIIJs with the long 50mm gun and 93 Panzer IIIs with the old gun. All of the Italian tanks were various marks of the Medium M13/40. In addition the Germans had 29 light tanks and the Italians 38.

Rommel knew that time was most definitely not on his side. Reconnaissance showed that the British were laying extensive minefields and thickening their defences, especially in the northern sector near the coast and in front of the Ruweisat Ridge. The British with their short supply lines were also winning the battle of the build-up and were growing

German Panzergrenadier counts down the seconds to the start of an attack. (IWM HU5624)

stronger by the day. The strengthening of the British defences ruled out any hope of making an easy breakthrough in the north, or across the Ruweisat Ridge. The south seemed to be the area most favourable for his attack. This sector of the line was not as heavily fortified, although Eighth Army troops were still busy constructing new defences and extending their minefields even as Rommel watched.

German intelligence had also identified that a large convoy bringing over 100,000 tons of weapons, tanks, equipment and stores was due to arrive at Suez in early September. Rommel, on the other hand, with his extended lines and difficulties in transporting material across the Mediterranean, was finding it hard to assemble an effective force. He had to attack soon or face an even stronger enemy. He therefore decided to launch a new attempt to reach the Delta around the period of the full moon which was due on 26 August.

The German field marshal decided to employ the tried and tested tactics he had used previously in the assault, opting for a night attack through the British southern flank and an advance 45 kilometres eastwards past Alam Halfa ridge so that by dawn he could unleash his Afrika Korps northwards round the rear of Eighth Army's positions. The right flank of his attack would be protected by all of the highly mobile German and Italian reconnaissance units. Guarding the left flank would be the Ariete and Littorio Armoured Divisions of Italian XX Corps, with the rested 90th Light Division moving on the extreme northern flank of the assault. Rommel had great confidence in his troops and most especially in the Afrika Korps. This plan seemed to be the most promising, but to ensure success it relied on surprise, speed and having sufficient supplies available to support a mobile attack. To gain surprise Rommel planned to assemble his armoured forces by night and camouflage them by day. To mask the direction of the attack, diversionary raids and smaller attacks would be made in the north by Italian infantry.

It was a good plan, but one that was obvious to the British. Auchinleck had already concluded that the enemy assault would most probably be in the south, with an armoured thrust driving eastwards then swinging up behind Alam Halfa, and had taken steps to counter it. ULTRA intercepts had also confirmed that this was Rommel's intention, so when Montgomery arrived in Egypt to take command of the situation he was presented with advance warning of his opponent's overall strategy. This removed Rommel's element of surprise.

The key to the battle would be the Alam Halfa Ridge. If the Germans could get past it to the east, they could shift northwards and meet the British armour on favourable ground, behind the bulk of Eighth Army's positions. If Montgomery's forces could hold the ridge, then Rommel would not dare move further eastwards towards the Suez Canal with the whole of Eighth Army dominating his lines of communications. Montgomery therefore strengthened his forces on and around the feature. He brought forward the newly arrived 44th Division and lined up two of its brigades – 131st and 133rd Brigades – along the ridge with all of its divisional artillery and anti-tank guns. On the western end he placed 22nd Armoured Brigade from 10th Armoured Division. Further west the defensive position about Alam Nayil was held by the New Zealand Division, strengthened by the addition of 132nd Brigade. Just to the north, at the eastern end of Ruweisat Ridge, was XXX Corps' reserve, the

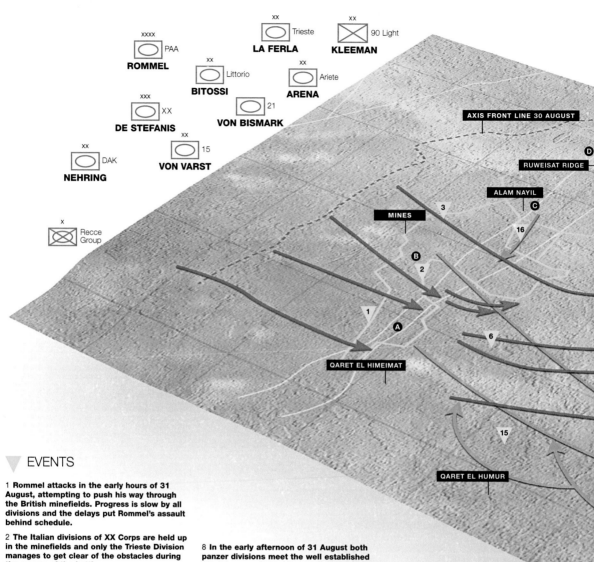

EVENTS

1 **Rommel attacks in the early hours of 31 August, attempting to push his way through the British minefields. Progress is slow by all divisions and the delays put Rommel's assault behind schedule.**

2 **The Italian divisions of XX Corps are held up in the minefields and only the Trieste Division manages to get clear of the obstacles during the course of the battle.**

3 **The 90th Light Division also has difficulty crossing the British minefields and takes most of the first day trying to reach Deir el Muhafid.**

4 **After fighting a delaying action against the DAK, 4th Light Armoured Brigade falls back into 7th Armoured Division's positions around Samaket Gaballa**

5 **The 7th Motor Brigade delays Italian XX Corps and the 90th Light Division in the minefield then withdraws to Samaket Gaballa to join the rest of 7th Armoured Division.**

6 **The 15th and 21st Panzer Divisions finally get through the minefields later than expected and the delay forces Rommel to modify his original plan of passing to the east of Alam El Halfa. He now decides to turn his armoured divisions north before Alam El Halfa Ridge and strike towards the sea between that feature and the Ruweisat Ridge.**

7 **Once the direction of Rommel's attack becomes clear to Gen Montgomery, the Eighth Army's commander counters it by bringing his 23rd Armoured Brigade south alongside 22nd Armoured Brigade.**

8 **In the early afternoon of 31 August both panzer divisions meet the well established 22nd Armoured Brigade and fight an intense battle against British artillery and anti-tank guns. Unable to break through the defensive cordon, the attacks are broken off in the evening.**

9 **Early on 1 September the Panzer divisions try again to get past Alam el Halfa by moving to the east of 22nd Armoured Brigade. 15th Panzer Division is then struck by 8th Armoured Brigade which is moving across to join 22nd Armoured Brigade. Both formations are forced to a halt.**

10 **Montgomery further strengthens the Alam el Halfa position on 1 September by moving South African 2nd Brigade from XXX Corps to the north of the ridge.**

11 **Late on 1 September Rommel decides that he will have to call off the attack and go over to the defensive.**

12 **The next day, 2 September, Montgomery brings forward 151st Brigade from 50th Division to begin exerting pressure on the DAK.**

13 **In the south, 7th Armoured Division mounts probing attacks on the German Reconnaissance Group and the flanks of DAK.**

14 **On 2 September, Rommel orders a gradual withdrawal of all formations back to positions to the west of the British minefields.**

15 **The 7th Armoured Division continues its harassing attacks on the retreating Axis forces.**

16 **On the night of 3/4 September, New Zealand 2nd Division attacks southwards from its positions towards Deir el Muassib to harass the Axis withdrawal and to close the gaps in the minefields. The attack is met by stiff opposition and, after a day's fighting, is called off, allowing Rommel's forces to return to their original positions.**

ALAM EL HALFA: ROMMEL'S LAST CHANCE

This was Rommel's last attempt to break through to the Nile valley and he was anxious to gain a quick victory with dwindling resources. For Montgomery it was his introduction to the North Africa campaign and his first battle with the Eighth Army.

Note: Gridlines are shown at intervals of 5 miles

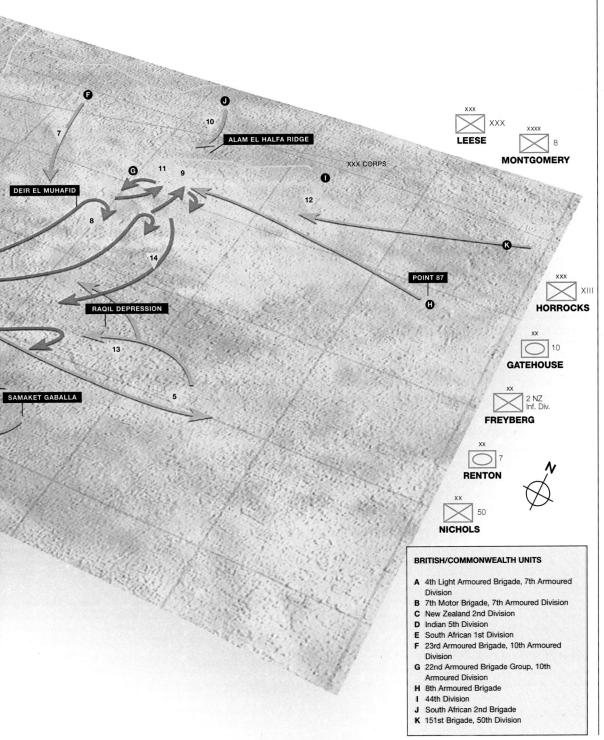

LEESE

MONTGOMERY

XXX CORPS

ALAM EL HALFA RIDGE

DEIR EL MUHAFID

RAQIL DEPRESSION

POINT 87

HORROCKS

GATEHOUSE

2 NZ
Inf. Div.

FREYBERG

SAMAKET GABALLA

RENTON

NICHOLS

N

BRITISH/COMMONWEALTH UNITS

A 4th Light Armoured Brigade, 7th Armoured
   Division
B 7th Motor Brigade, 7th Armoured Division
C New Zealand 2nd Division
D Indian 5th Division
E South African 1st Division
F 23rd Armoured Brigade, 10th Armoured
   Division
G 22nd Armoured Brigade Group, 10th
   Armoured Division
H 8th Armoured Brigade
I 44th Division
J South African 2nd Brigade
K 151st Brigade, 50th Division

Captured Soviet 75mm gun used by the Germans in an anti-tank role. It may have knocked out the burning tank in the background. (IWM MH5862)

23rd Armoured Brigade. Monty planned to wait and see which way Rommel moved before committing the 23rd Armoured Brigade against him. Further to the east, around Point 87, was 10th Armoured Division's 8th Armoured Brigade. Holding the line in the south was 7th Armoured Division, with 4th Light Armoured Brigade and 7th Motor Brigade. Montgomery planned for these two brigades to try to hold any enemy attack, but to withdraw in the face of the German advance into positions around Samaket Gaballa. It was important that the division was kept intact and not overwhelmed by superior forces, for once the Afrika Korps had moved east, the 7th Armoured Division was to harry its flanks. To the north, XXX Corps was to hold the line with the three Dominion divisions already in place and absorb any diversionary attacks.

The element of speed required for Rommel's success was down to the Afrika Korps. It had to move its tanks through the British minefields and into open desert before dawn. Rommel was confident that it would. The third element essential for success, good supplies, and more importantly large quantities of petrol, was beyond Rommel's control. He had been promised adequate fuel for the attack, but the full moon of the 26 August came and began to wane while his fuel bunkers contained just the standard two days' worth of fuel. Nothing extra had reached Egypt or indeed North Africa. The supply situation for Panzerarmee Afrika was somewhat eased when Kesselring authorized the transfer of 1,500 tons of fuel from the Luftwaffe, enough for four days' usage. Further relief was promised by Cavallero, who insisted that a number of petrol tankers were due to arrive in Benghazi and Tripoli on 30 August. On these slim promises, Rommel steeled himself for battle and ordered the assault to go ahead as planned.

Rommel's attack got off to a poor start during the night of 30–31 August. Shortly after passing the eastern boundary of the Axis minefields

the attacking troops came up against unsuspected belts of British mines of such depth that the advance slowed almost to a halt. Intense artillery fire descended on Rommel's engineers and infantry as they tried to deal with an estimated 150,000 mines and booby traps which littered the sector of the attack. Whilst its men were engaged in the operation, the Afrika Korps was hit by relays of heavy bombers disrupting progress through the belt of obstacles. The two brigades of 7th Armoured Division fought well in defence and staged a controlled withdrawal as planned. The result was that none of the attacking formations had reached their appointed objectives by dawn. This delay in the timetable of the advance had ensured that the British were able to plot the route of the attack and be well prepared to receive the expected armoured thrust.

As news began to filter into Rommel's HQ the picture looked bleak. He acknowledged that the British had defended with extraordinary stubbornness and achieved a setback in his plan. He had hoped that by dawn his tanks would be 45 kilometres east of the minefields, ready to swing north towards the sea. Further bad news reached the army commander when he learned that GenMaj von Bismarck, commander of 21st Panzer Division had been killed by a mine and that Gen der Pz Nehring had been wounded in an air attack on his Afrika Korps. Rommel now considered abandoning the offensive, but decided to press on when he heard from Oberst Bayerlein, Nehring's Chief of Staff who had taken over command of the Afrika Korps, that the tanks were through the mines and driving east.

The delays suffered in the minefields and by air raids caused Rommel to reconsider his original plan. With the British alerted and ready, a wide sweep to the east, passing to the south of Alam Halfa Ridge, would expose his right flanks to the 7th Armoured Division and the 10th Armoured Division which he knew was in the north. He now decided to turn left before he got to Alam Halfa, much earlier than previously intended. New objectives were set: Point 132 on the ridge for the Afrika Korps and Point 102 at Alam Bueit for XX Corps. Then his forces would drive northwards passing behind the Ruweisat Ridge towards the coast road. But first the

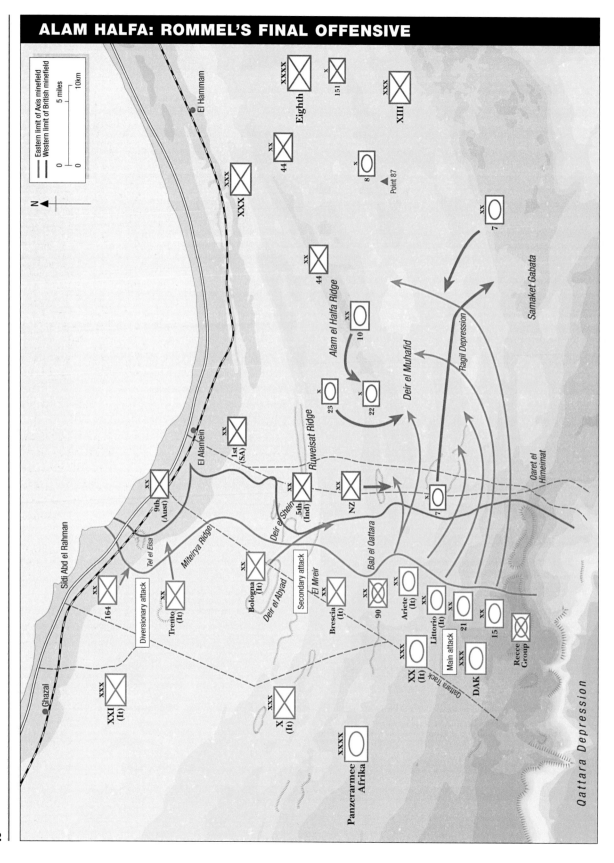

Eastern limit of Axis minefield
Western limit of British minefield

0 5 miles
0 10km

N

El Hammam

XXXX Eighth
x 151
XXX XIII

xx 44
x 8
Point 87

XXX XXX

xx 7

xx 44 Alam el Halfa Ridge

xx 10

Samaket Gabata

x 23
x 22

Deir el Muhafid

Ragil Depression

El Alamein
1st (SA) xx

Ruweisat Ridge

xx 54th (Ind)
xx NZ
x 7

Qaret el Himeimat

9th (Aust) xx

Sidi Abd el Rahman
Tel el Eisa
Miteirya Ridge
Deir el Shein
Bab el Qattara

164 xx
Diversionary attack
Trento (It) xx
Bologna (It) xx
Deir el Abyad
Secondary attack
El Mreir
Brescia (It) xx
90 xx
Ariete (It) xx
Littorio (It) xx
21 xx
15 xx
Recce Group

Main attack
XX (It)
DAK XXX
Qattara Track

Ghazal

XXI (It) XXX

X (It) XXX

Panzerarmee Afrika XXXX

Qattara Depression

A dead crewman lies beside his
knocked-out Panzer III tank.
(IWM E16494)

advance had to halt to refuel and take on ammunition. It was 1300hrs
before it got going again.

Montgomery was pleased with the way things were shaping; the attack
had come in just where it had been anticipated. The minefields were
slowing down the advance as planned and throwing many of the Axis
units into disarray. None of Italian XX Corps' divisions had managed to
break free of the obstacles and 90th Light Division was virtually halted
around Deir el Munassib. Best of all, the Afrika Korps was identified south
of Alam Halfa and its direction of advance was aimed at the western end
of the ridge itself. Montgomery could now confidently bring 23rd
Armoured Brigade southwards to a position between 22nd Armoured
Brigade and the New Zealanders. Rommel was being lured onto the hull-
down tanks and anti-tank guns that were blocking his path.

The battle now took the course that Montgomery had hoped for.
Both 15th and 21st Panzer Divisions ran into the defensive positions of
the two British Armoured Brigades under the guns of division and corps
artillery. Tank and anti-tank fire raked the advancing Germans and did
great damage. Try as they might, the British armour could not be
enticed out of their hull-down positions. It was now the Germans' turn
to suffer the consequences of trying to overwhelm well established anti-
tank guns and armour. When the light began to fade the attack was
called off. The panzers withdrew to replenish their strength from
dwindling stocks of fuel and ammunition.

Throughout the night, just as they had done during the long day, the
Desert Air Force bombed and strafed the enemy. Flares lit up the night sky
and the bright light etched out soft-topped transport, armour and guns
on the bare desert below, exposing them to medium bombers and low
flying fighter-bombers. None of the Axis troops were allowed any rest, for

The aftermath of the Alam Halfa action. British troops inspect the wrecked transport left on the battlefield by the Afrika Korps. (IWM E16651)

no sooner had one raid finished when another started. They lay all night in the sand, suffering the strain of waiting for the next bomb to fall.

Early the next day 15th Panzer Division tried to work around the eastern flank of 22nd Armoured Brigade. The move was frustrated by 8th Armoured Brigade moving across from Point 87 to join up with 22nd Armoured Brigade. Both sides were forced to a halt by supporting anti-tank fire. That day 21st Panzer Division did very little, frustrated by lack of fuel and strafed by artillery fire from the ridge. On the left flank of the Afrika Korps the Ariete and Littorio Divisions were still struggling to get clear of the minefields under continuous fire from the New Zealand Division. The Trieste Division did a little better, but still could not free itself from the artillery fire. Further north the 90th Light Division crawled forward past Munassib, never likely to get into the battle proper. By the end of the day, Rommel issued the order to his formations to go over to the defensive, dig themselves in and prepare for the next night of bombing.

Ever cautious, Montgomery now moved more formations to the Alam Halfa area. Now that all of the enemy's main force was committed, he was determined that they would get no further. He told XXX Corps to thin out its line and moved the South African 2nd Brigade further south to a position just north of the ridge. He also shifted Indian 5th Brigade southwards and brought it under command of Freyberg's New Zealand

Division. Super cautious, he then gave orders for 151st Brigade of 50th Division to cease its work as airfield protection back in the Delta and to come forward to the eastern end of the Alam Halfa Ridge. Rommel was now well and truly boxed in, for in the south, 7th Armoured Division was beginning to make sorties against his exposed flanks.

This was now the time for Montgomery to strike back and drive across Rommel's lines of communication to engineer a resounding defeat. The reinforcement of the New Zealand Division with Indian 5th Brigade came with a warning to LtGen Freyberg to get ready to attack southwards from Alam Nayil towards Himeimat. In the north, on 1 September Australian 9th Division carried out an operation west of Tel el Eisa and attacked German 164th Division, capturing 140 prisoners. This long-prepared move was planned to bring alarm to the Axis camp and to stress the vulnerability of their forces, strung out as they were across the desert.

Overhead fighters and bombers continued to plague the Afrika Korps. Joining with the Desert Air Force were a few squadrons of Mitchell bombers from the USAAF. They made 111 sorties on 1 September to join with the 372 flown by the RAF. That night they were active again over the Afrika Korps and included a few 4,000lb bombs in their loads with devastating effect.

Rommel knew that his offensive had failed. He had been held by a superior force arrayed on ground of its own choosing. He had also been let down by his superiors. Marshal Cavellero's promise of 5,000 tons of petrol failed to materialize: 2,600 tons of it had been sunk in the Mediterranean and 1,500 tons were still on the dockside in Italy. Just 900 tons were landed and much of that was consumed by transport on its long journey to the front. Kesselring's assurance of 1,500 tons of Luftwaffe fuel to be delivered by air was also a hollow gesture. Only a fraction of it arrived. On 2 September, Rommel ordered a gradual withdrawal of all formations back to the western edge of the British minefields.

Rommel was puzzled by Montgomery's tactics. He knew that the British had assembled a powerful armoured force between Alam Halfa and Bab el Qattara, but it had remained stationary in its assembly area. The impression he gained of the new British commander was 'of a very cautious man who was not prepared to take any sort of risk.' Montgomery was indeed acting cautiously. He judged Eighth Army to be unready to take on the task of a possible chase and ordered that the enemy was to be harassed vigorously, but the only staged attack was the one to be launched by LtGen Freyberg's division. This itself was to be limited to the closing of the minefield gaps behind the Axis forces and was not due to take place before the night of 3/4 September, almost two days after Rommel had begun his withdrawal.

Monty's counterattack finally began with diversionary raids by 6th New Zealand Division at 2300hrs on 3 September. These roused the enemy who met the advancing infantry of 132nd Brigade with mortar and machine-gun fire disrupting its advance, although a similar attack by New Zealand 5th Brigade did reach its initial objectives. Strong fighting went on throughout the night as the Italians and Germans fought to prevent the gaps being closed. Progress was poor and shortly after midday on 4 September the enemy came back at the New Zealand Division in a fierce counterattack. This was successfully turned aside,

**TANKS AND MOTORIZED INFANTRY FROM 15TH PANZER
DIVISION ATTACK TOWARDS ALAM HALFA RIDGE ON
1 SEPTEMBER** (pages 56–57)

GFM Rommel's last attempt to break through Eighth Army's
lines at El Alamein and drive on towards the Nile Delta was
delayed by the strength and depth of British minefields.
When his Afrika Korps finally emerged from the eastern
limit of the obstacles and manoeuvred to get behind the
main British positions, Rommel was forced to try to swing
his armour around the western end of the Alam Halfa Ridge
to make up for lost time. Montgomery tracked this
movement and brought 23rd Armoured Brigade southwards
to a position between 22nd Armoured Brigade and the New
Zealanders to block the move. Rommel's panzers had been
lured onto a mass of hull-down tanks and anti-tank guns
blocking his path. The battle then took the course that
Montgomery had hoped for. Both 15th and 21st Panzer
Divisions had to face the defensive positions of the two
British brigades and the 44th Division. They were caught
by a welter of fire from division and corps artillery, which
raked the advancing Afrika Korps with tank and anti-tank
shells. Panzers and Panzergrenadiers suffered
considerably trying to overwhelm these well-established
guns without being able to entice the British armour out
of their hull-down positions. The Battlescene shows tanks
of the 15th Panzer Division attacking towards Alam Halfa

Ridge on 31 August through the barrage of British fire.
At this stage of the campaign, 15th Panzer Division had
perfected its mobility and always attacked with infantry
support. The troops of the motorized 115th
Panzergrenadier Regiment were carried forward in SdKfz
251 half-track armoured personnel carriers (1) and trucks,
which allowed them to immediately exploit any gains made
by the armour. Amongst the division were a few of the
improved Panzer IV tanks (2) with the long 75mm gun
known to the British as a 'MarkIV Special'. This up-gunned
tank was master of the battlefield, outperforming all other
tanks. Unfortunately for Rommel, only a few of them were
available to the Afrika Korps for Alam Halfa and the bulk
of his armour consisted of older Panzer IIIs and short-
barrelled Panzer IVs. When the new Panzer IVs finally did
appear in North Africa in significant numbers, the Allies
had by then also received a new tank with comparable
performance in the shape of the Sherman. The
15th Panzer Division was formed from the 33rd Infantry
Division which had taken part in the campaign in France
in 1940. It arrived in North Africa in 1941 with one panzer
regiment (the 8th) and two Panzergrenadier regiments
(the 104th and the 115th) and became the founding
division of the Afrika Korps. A short time later it gave up
its 104th Panzergrenadier Regiment to join with 5th Panzer
Regiment to the form the new 21st Panzer Division.
(Howard Gerrard)

then a second attack took place a few hours later. Artillery fire backed up by day bombers helped to break up both assaults. The enemy's fierce reaction convinced Freyberg that a renewed attack by his division would not succeed and he requested permission for a complete withdrawal. This was granted by both Horrocks and Montgomery.

The attempt to close the minefields and to show at least some sign of aggressive action had failed. Even the British official history admits that 'it had caused the enemy no more than passing concern.' It did, however, give the New Zealand Division itself some cause for concern, for it lost 275 men, including the capture of its 6th Brigade's commander, Brig Clifton. The 132nd Brigade fared even worse, with 697 killed, wounded and missing, among whom was its commander, Brig Robertson. It was a very disappointing outcome for such a high number of casualties. Total British casualties after almost a week of fighting amounted to 1,750 killed, wounded and missing. The Italians lost 1,051 men and the Germans 1,859. The Germans had 38 tanks destroyed and the Italians 11, while the British lost 67. In the air, losses in aircraft from all causes were British 68, Italian 5 and German 36.

The Battle of Alam Halfa ended with Panzerarmee Afrika withdrawing all of its formations to the western side of the British minefields unmolested, except for some light actions fought by the 7th and 10th Armoured Divisions following at a safe distance. Montgomery even left Axis forces in possession of the high ground at Himeimat, claiming that he rather liked them to overlook his southern front so that they could see the bogus preparations being made for his coming offensive and perhaps believe that his main attack would be launched in the south.

EL ALAMEIN: THE ATTACK

Gen Montgomery was quite satisfied with the outcome of the Alam Halfa battle. He felt that the application of his tactics had demonstrated that the revitalized Eighth Army under his command was more than capable of defeating Rommel. As soon as the battle was over, all of Montgomery's energy was concentrated on his proposed offensive to break Panzerarmee Afrika. Every man in Eighth Army, from its commander down to its rank and file, now applied himself to the preparations for the coming battle.

The first task was to replace and strengthen the minefields that were lost in the German breakthrough. Next, a programme of training rolled out through the army as each formation rehearsed the techniques that were required for the task that had been allocated to it in the attack. Much new equipment was arriving in Egypt and troops were required to adjust to the new demands placed upon them. Units were reshuffled to bring them under their appropriate command; Montgomery insisted that divisions must fight as divisions with all of the support units that were proper to them. There would be no brigade groups as had been common in the past, except in the case of the Greek and French contingents. They would still operate independently with their own support units.

One of the first things that Montgomery did when he arrived in Egypt was to create a mobile corps of armour which he termed his *corps de chasse*.

A British film cameraman takes a look inside a knocked out Italian M13/40 Italian tank. The turret is facing to the rear. (IWM E14556)

He envisaged that the formation would be the British equivalent of the Afrika Korps; an armoured strike force that could exploit any breakthrough made in the enemy lines. He chose X Corps for this task and moved LtGen Lumsden across from 1st Armoured Division to take over the reformed corps. Lumsden was not Monty's first choice for the command; he would have preferred to have someone he knew in charge of the corps, but pressure was applied by Alexander to employ one of the existing Eighth Army commanders who had both desert and armoured experience.

Montgomery brought into X Corps the 1st, 10th and the newly arrived 8th Armoured Divisions, together with the 2nd New Zealand Division which had been reorganized by the addition of British 9th Armoured Brigade. The 7th Armoured Division remained with Horrocks' XIII Corps.

Many changes now took place amongst the senior officers, for there was a great weeding out of unsuitable, over-age and ineffective commanders. The biggest change was the removal of LtGen Ramsden as commander of XXX Corps. He was replaced by a newcomer from England, LtGen Oliver Leese, from Guards Armoured Division. MajGen Renton left 7th Armoured Division to be replaced by MajGen A.F. Harding who moved over from his post as Deputy Chief of Staff in Cairo. Lower down the chain of command, more new men with new ideas were promoted to replace those that Montgomery deemed to be out of touch or tired.

There was a great deal of pressure being applied to Alexander to persuade Montgomery to launch his attack sooner rather than later. Churchill was pushing for a resounding victory over Rommel before the proposed Anglo-American landings in Morocco and Algeria took place. These were planned for early November and it was important that the Vichy French in those countries, and in Tunisia, were influenced in the Allies' favour before the Americans arrived. An Axis defeat in North Africa would go some way in persuading the French colonials not to oppose the landings. It was also important that fresh convoys got through to the besieged island of Malta whose population was near to starvation. These convoys could not sail until the enemy had been cleared from airfields in nearby Cyrenaica. Churchill pressed for the attack to be made in late September, but Montgomery would not be swayed from his target launch date of mid-October. He was determined not to move until he was absolutely ready.

On 3 September the promised shipment of 300 American Sherman tanks arrived at Suez to be dispersed amongst the armoured brigades, usually one squadron per armoured regiment. The build-up of armour continued with British-built tanks also arriving in greater numbers. By the start of the offensive Eighth Army's effective tank strength ready for action was 1,038, comprising 252 Shermans, 170 Grants, 294 Crusaders, 119 Stuarts, 194 Valentines, six Matildas and three Churchills. In addition there were around 200 of all types available as replacements. Also arriving were large numbers of the new 6-pdr anti-tank gun and more of the smaller 2-pdr gun. At the start of the battle there were 554 2-pdr and 849 6-pdr anti-tank guns in operation. This meant that all of the Royal Artillery anti-tank regiments were now equipped with the effective 6-pdr guns, each more than capable of dealing with Axis armour. In support, the Royal Artillery had 52 medium guns and 832, 25-pdr field pieces. The fire power of Eighth Army had more than doubled during the critical weeks leading up to Montgomery's offensive. Supplies were plentiful, vast quantities of fuel and ammunition were available from stocks in the Delta and were being delivered along short lines of communication well served by road and rail. These improvements, coupled with the changes in command and the reorganization of units and formations, brought an air of renewed confidence and vigour amongst the 195,000 men who made up the fighting strength of Eighth Army.

It only remained for Montgomery to formulate a plan that would break Rommel's line and force Panzerarmee Afrika into retreat. With no room to manoeuvre a mobile striking force of armour around the enemy's flank, Montgomery was constrained to force a passage right through his main defensive zones. He therefore decided that his main attack would be made in the north by XXX Corps, with a subsidiary assault in the south by XIII Corps. Deception plans would be used to make the enemy believe that the southern attack was in fact the main effort, for it would be strong enough to prevent the enemy moving troops to reinforce the northern sector. Montgomery's original plan relied on the armour of Lumsden's X Corps helping to carve out a passage through the German defences, but reluctance which verged on mutiny by the armoured commanders swayed Monty into changing his intentions. He settled on a plan which would rely on simultaneous attacks by four infantry divisions to help clear routes through which the armoured divisions could advance. The armoured divisions would then themselves clear two corridors through the minefields passable for tanks. Then the infantry would widen their breaches to the north and south by methodically destroying enemy troops, 'crumbling' away the Axis defenders by overwhelming artillery fire and local attacks. Rommel could not stand idle and watch his defences disintegrate; he would have to commit his armour to help save his infantry. The British tank force would then manoeuvre through the breaches to meet the counterattack by the Panzer divisions.

A British sergeant looking out across the Qattara Depression. This vast area of soft sand was thought to be impenetrable to most vehicles and therefore anchored the southern end of the El Alamein defence line. (IWM E16399)

The overwhelming strength of the land forces that Montgomery was able to put in the field, was similarly matched by the British effort in the air. Air Vice-Marshal Coningham had 104 squadrons at his disposal from the RAF, Dominion and USAAF units. He could put 530 serviceable aircraft aloft against the 350 serviceable aircraft available to Axis air forces (150 German and 200 Italian). Coningham planned to attack the enemy's airfields by day and night and to provide fighter cover over the army's forward area. He would also provide constant reconnaissance over the enemy positions before the attack while at the same time interdicting any Axis attempts to spy on British preparations. Once the battle began, Coningham intended to provide constant ground support as required. There was to be complete army and air force co-operation. Even the Royal Navy was to participate in the action, planning disruptive demonstrations along the coast to simulate landings in the rear of Rommel's forces.

To the west of Eighth Army, ensconced behind thick minefields, Panzerarmee Afrika was not so full of confidence. Visions of capturing Cairo and the Suez Canal had faded from their memories. The Germans and Italians waited in their exposed dugouts sure in the knowledge that the big attack was coming. They had no illusions about what was in store for them. They knew that their once mobile army had been reduced to a static role, just waiting for the enemy to strike. Most of the Italians were now longing for the end of the war. Successful British attacks by sea and air against shipping had meant that supplies were short, ammunition was scarce and fuel was rationed. Replacements in manpower had not kept pace with losses, with the inevitable result that all formations were below strength. To make matters worse, their inspiring commander was gone, invalided home to Germany for a rest.

Rommel's health had deteriorated during the campaign. He had pushed himself hard for two years and had taken little rest; by the end of the Alam Halfa battle he was near to collapse. His doctor ordered him home for at least six weeks' leave to recuperate. Rommel was replaced by *Gen der Kavallerie* Georg Stumme who had commanded Rommel's old 7th Panzer Division and then XXXX Panzer Korps on the Russian Front.

Before he left, Rommel spent the first two weeks of September reorganizing his formations to meet the coming attack which he expected to take place early in October. He knew that the British had overwhelming superiority both on land and in the air but would not choose to fight a mobile battle against his Afrika Korps. He was therefore forced to base his defence on a static fortified line against which he knew the British would use their massed artillery. The battle would start with an infantry attack which would have to carve a way through the defences for their tanks to follow. As a result Rommel knew that his plan of defence was simple: the line must be made as strong as possible with the main positions capable of holding out against the heaviest assault long enough for the Panzer divisions to come to their aid. He also supposed that the initial assault would be made at several places, with Montgomery looking to exploit the most favourable penetration.

The Axis line was to be held by Italian troops interlaced with German units. Italian and German formations were superimposed on top of each other right down to battalion level to stiffen the Italian resolve and bring German expertise into the defence. Rommel kept his two main tank formations to the rear of the defences, with 15th Panzer Division in the northern sector and 21st Panzer Division in the south. De Stefanis' XX Corps was split up, with the Littorio Armoured Division in front of 15th Panzer and the Ariete in the south together with 21st Panzer. In reserve by the coast, but well to the west of the main line, were 90th Light Division and the Trieste Motorized Division. From the coast down to the Miteirya Ridge the main line was held by German 164th Division and Gen Gloria's Italian XXI Corps, with Trento Division overlapping the positions held by the 164th. From there to Deir el Shein and Ruweisat Ridge was covered

Italian signal men repairing a break in the communications line. All lines had to be laid across open ground and the passage of tanks and lorries over them caused breaks that needed almost constant attention. Most contact between formations in forward areas had to be by radio. (Ufficio Storico Esercito Rome)

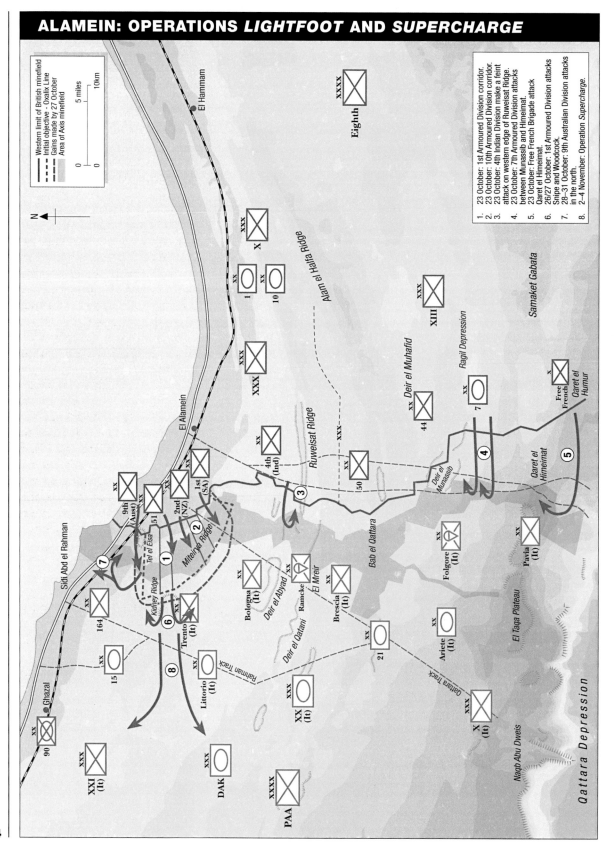

Western limit of British minefield
Initial objective - Oxalix Line
Gains made by 27 October
Area of Axis minefield

0   5 miles
0   5   10km

N

1. 23 October: 1st Armoured Division corridor.
2. 23 October: 10th Armoured Division corridor.
3. 23 October: 4th Indian Division make a feint attack on western edge of Ruweisat Ridge.
4. 23 October: 7th Armoured Division attacks between Munassib and Himeimat.
5. 23 October: Free French Brigade attack Qaret el Himeimat.
6. 26/27 October: 1st Armoured Division attacks Snipe and Woodcock.
7. 28–31 October: 9th Australian Division attacks in the north.
8. 2–4 November: Operation *Supercharge*.

El Hammam

Eighth

Alam el Halfa Ridge

X

XX 1   10

XXX

Samaket Gabata

XXX XIII

Ragil Depression

Deir el Muhafid

El Alamein

Ruweisat Ridge

4th (Ind)   XXX

xx 7

xx 44

Free French

Qaret el Humur

150

Dair el Munassib

Qaret el Himeimat

9th (Aust)   51   2nd (NZ)   1st (SA)

Tel el Eisa   Miteiriya Ridge

Kidney Ridge

Sidi Abd el Rahman

Bab el Qattara

Folgore (It)

Pavia (It)

164

Trento (It)

Bologna (It)   Deir el Abyad   Ramcke   El Mreir   Brescia (It)

Deir el Qatani

El Taqa Plateau

15   Rahman Track   Littorio (It)   XX (It)   Qattara Track   21   Ariete (It)

Naqb Abu Dweis

X (It)

Ghazal   90   XXI (It)   DAK   PAA

Qattara Depression

by the Bologna Division. To the south of these positions was Gen Frattini's X Corps, with the Brescia Division around Bab el Qattara. Both the Bologna and the Brescia Divisions were 'sandwiched' with battalions of Ramcke's Parachute Brigade. The remainder of the line southwards to Qaret el Himeimat contained the Folgore Parachute Division and the Pavia Division.

The Axis defences were designed in depth, beginning with a thin screen of outposts on the edge of the forward minefields, with some section posts actually in the minefields themselves. The minefields were strewn with both anti-tank and anti-personnel mines, linked together with booby traps and other obstacles. A German report just before the battle suggested that there were 445,000 mines in the Axis minefields, about 14,000 of which were antipersonnel type. These advance positions would contain a company of infantry with a few anti-tank guns and machine guns. The lightly held zones located well forward enabled the main line of defence and the heavier anti-tank guns to be placed to the rear, further away from British artillery. About two kilometres behind these advance positions was the principal minefield belt with strong defensive locations along its front edge. Each Axis battalion would hold a sector of the line about one-and-a-half kilometres long and five kilometres deep. The main position would contain the bulk of the anti-tank and machine guns. The depth of the line from the forward positions to the rear of the defensive zone was between four and seven kilometres. Behind this were the heavy artillery and then the Panzer divisions, waiting to bring their fire onto any possible penetration. It was important for Rommel to confine the British within this defended zone. Rommel knew that if the British armour ever managed to break out into the open, then the battle would be virtually lost.

Rommel relied on his instinct that the British would attack in their usual manner, saturating the forward positions with devastating artillery fire and then putting in an infantry assault. This would give ample warning to the main defence line of the direction and strength of the attack. By the time the main line was reached, the initial surprise would have been lost and the impetus of the attack would be starting to wane. The advancing infantry would then be met with the strongest part of the defences. Any attempt to push armour through at this point would be countered by the anti-tank screen which in all probability would have been missed by the artillery bombardment. As the battle progressed, any likely penetration could then be countered by shifting into that sector the whole or part of one of the armoured divisions.

The effective tank strength of the Panzer divisions was well below their peak, with 249 German and 278 Italian main tanks and just 20 light tanks available for action. In anti-tank guns, the Axis forces contained 68 7.65cm guns, and 290 5cm Pak 38s. Of the potent dual-role 8.8cm flak guns, Rommel never had enough and never stopped asking for more. At the start of the battle 19th Flak Division deployed 86 of these weapons in the forward area and a further 52 in the rear areas for anti-aircraft defence of the airfields and ports. The fighting strength of Panzerarmee Afrika was around 104,000, of which 54,000 were Italian and 50,000 German.

While Montgomery had been switching many of his senior commanders because of a perceived lack of ability, Rommel was obliged to change some of his for more depressing reasons. The wounded Nehring was replaced by GenLt Wilhelm Ritter von Thoma as head of the Afrika

Korps. Von Thoma came from Russia with a growing reputation as an armoured commander. GenMaj Heinz von Randow replaced the dead von Bismarck at the head of 21st Panzer Division and GenLt Graf von Sponeck succeeded the wounded Kleeman in 90th Light Division. Such an influx of new senior commanders did little to improve confidence amongst Axis forces, but it was the loss of their lucky talisman, GFM Rommel, that hit them most.

Before Rommel left for his rest in Austria, he met with Marshal Cavellero and demanded that shipments of supplies to Panzerarmee Afrika be increased. He asked for at least 30,000 tons to be delivered in September and 35,000 tons in October. Cavellero reassured him that every effort would be made to meet these totals. On his way to Germany Rommel repeated his demands to Mussolini and then again to Hitler and Göring when he arrived in Berlin a few days later, but was left with a feeling that little would be done.

The battle was set to begin on the night of 23 October. Lined up that night along the edge of the British minefields were XXX and XIII Corps. LtGen Leese's XXX Corps was on the right with, from north to south, 9th Australian Division, 51st (Highland) Division, 2nd New Zealand Division, 1st South African Division and 4th Indian Division. These were in the line from the coast to the south of the Ruweisat Ridge. From there to the Qattara Depression was Horrocks' XIII Corps containing 50th Division, 44th Division, 7th Armoured Division and 1st French Brigade. Lumsden's X Corps, with 1st and 10th Armoured Divisions, was in the rear of XXX Corps near the coast. The recently arrived 8th Armoured Division was destined not to take part in the battle as a division. It had been split, with its 24th Armoured Brigade under the command of 10th Armoured Division and the remainder of the division grouped together into a formation called 'Hammerforce' and placed under the command of 1st Armoured Division.

Montgomery's final orders for the offensive, code named 'Lightfoot', called for three simultaneous attacks to be made. In the north, XXX Corps would penetrate the enemy line and form a bridgehead beyond the main Axis defence zone, advancing to a forward position code named 'Oxalic', then assist X Corps to pass through. In the south, XIII Corps would penetrate the enemy positions near Munassib and pass the 7th Armoured Division through towards Jebel Kalakh. The division was told

Italian Semovente 75/18 self-propelled gun. This vehicle consisted of a turretless medium M40 tank chassis mounted with a 75mm gun, which made it a very potent, but unreliable, weapon. (Ufficio Storico Esercito Rome)

not to get itself into a slogging match, but to preserve its strength for later mobile operations, its main task to threaten the enemy in order to keep his armour in the south. Finally, XIII Corps would use the 1st French Brigade to secure the Qaret el Himeimat and the El Taqa plateau. Both XXX and XIII Corps were then to begin the crumbling operations to grind down the enemy infantry and draw the Panzers onto the armoured divisions and the massed anti-tank guns. If the enemy armoured divisions failed to come forward to meet the challenge, 1st and 10th Armoured Divisions were to seek positions from which they could prevent the enemy from interfering with XXX Corps' crumbling operations.

The main weight of Eighth Army's assault was with XXX Corps. Four of its divisions were to attack Axis minefields and defences then help carve out two cleared corridors for the armoured divisions. On the right, 9th Australian Division would attack eastwards from Tel El Eisa; on its left, 51st Division would clear a path towards Kidney Ridge. Both of these divisions would cover the ground of 1st Armoured Division's northern corridor through the enemy minefields. South of these divisions, 2nd New Zealand Division would clear towards the western end of the Miteiriya Ridge and 1st South African Division would attack across the main part of the ridge. These would then cover the southern corridor through the minefields for 10th Armoured Division. On the extreme left of XXX Corps, the 4th Indian Division would take no major part in the opening attack, but would make threatening and diversionary raids from the western end of Ruweisat Ridge.

The battle opened with a tremendous artillery barrage at 2140hrs on 23 October. At first the guns opened up on the known locations of all enemy gun sites with anti-battery fire. This fire then switched to the forward edge of the enemy defences. As the infantry attacked, the artillery laid down a rolling barrage in front of them, lifting by measured amounts as the infantry moved forward. For the first time in the desert, there were sufficient anti-tank guns protecting the infantry to allow all of the 25-pdr weapons to be massed together under centralized command in their proper role as field guns. Medium and heavy guns of the Royal Artillery were added to produce the greatest concentrated barrage since the First World War. Ammunition supplies were unrestricted allowing the

guns to fire at a prodigious rate. In the following twelve days of fighting, the 834 field guns fired altogether over one million rounds, an average of 102 rounds per gun per day. The rates for the other guns were even higher; 133 rounds for the 4.5in guns and 157 for the 5.5in weapons.

The Desert Air Force added its weight to the bombardment by bombing known enemy gun positions and those German and Italian guns which returned fire. Specially equipped Wellington bombers also flew overhead, jamming the radio-telephony channels of the Axis forces in an effort to disrupt enemy communications. These measures effectively blocked off radio traffic for a period, adding to the confusion at Panzerarmee's HQ as to the size and direction of the attack.

The four divisions of XXX Corps attacked together on a 16km front, each with two brigades forward. Each division had one regiment of Valentine tanks from 23rd Armoured Brigade in support, except Freyberg's New Zealanders who had the whole of 9th Armoured Brigade under command. The four formations advanced across a kilometre of no-man's-land and then began their attack through six kilometres of enemy-held territory towards their objective, phase line 'Oxalic'.

Nearest the sea, the Australians attacked with 26th Brigade on the right and the 20th Brigade on the left. Its third brigade, 24th Brigade, made noisy feints towards the coast in an effort to draw fire. The right brigade reached 'Oxalic' after some fierce encounters with the enemy, but 20th Brigade was stopped about a kilometre short by stiff resistance. The Australian Division endured the same pattern of events that was being experienced by other attacking divisions. The first minefield and line of defence was crossed with no great difficulty, just as Rommel expected them to be. But, as the two brigades pushed on into the main German defence line and the second minefield, enemy resistance increased.

On the left of the Australians, the Highlanders of 51st Division advanced on a two-brigade front with 153rd Brigade on the right and 154th Brigade on the left. Each brigade moved with one battalion forward and the other two ready to follow up. They set out to the stirring sounds of regimental pipers marching at the head of the battalions. In order to maintain the momentum, when each intermediate phase line was reached, the

Royal Engineer mine-clearance teams were amongst the most valuable troops on the battlefield. The numbers of mines laid in front of both opposing armies was prodigious and little forward progress could be made until they had been lifted to allow tanks and vehicles to pass through. (IWM E16226)

forward battalion paused while the battalion to its rear leapfrogged over into the lead. This procedure was repeated across other phase lines towards 'Oxalic'. The Highland Division had the most difficult task of XXX Corps, for its final objectives covered a width double the front of its start line. There was also a larger number of defended localities to be overcome, each of which had to be eliminated before the advance could continue. Progress at first was good, but it was gradually slowed down by the large numbers of casualties that the division was suffering. By dawn the Highland Division had not penetrated the enemy's main defence line. The delays and difficulties met during the advance meant that the mine clearance teams hoping to open a corridor for 1st Armoured Division were delayed.

The 2nd New Zealand Division began its attack on the western end of Miteirya Ridge also on a two-brigade front, with just one battalion at a time in the lead. LtGen Freyberg had decided to use his two infantry brigades to fight their way to the ridge before introducing the full strength of 9th Armoured Brigade to pass through and get beyond the high ground. He wanted to save as much of his weight as he could for this final stage. The plan worked well and the New Zealander infantry, despite heavy casualties, cleared a way through the minefields to allow Brig Currie to get his tanks on the crest of the ridge just before dawn. The coming of daylight, however, brought accurate enemy fire which forced the armour back on to the reverse slopes.

MajGen Pienaar's 1st South African Division advanced in much the same method as the New Zealanders. The infantry penetrated the minefields and cleared a way for some armoured support and the division was able, with great effort, to get onto the eastern end of the ridge. Difficulty was met in trying to get vehicles and heavy weapons forward which limited the strength of the division's positions. It had hoped to get beyond the ridge and allow armoured cars and the tanks of 8th RTR to exploit the left hand of XXX Corps attack, but enemy resistance forced it to dig in along the ridge. Just a little further south, Indian 4th Division made threatening raids near Ruweisat Ridge to confuse the enemy with regard to the length of the main British attack.

In the main, the first twelve hours of XXX Corps' attack had been fairly successful. LtGen Leese had got his divisions through most of the minefields and well into the enemy's positions. Best of all, he had troops on the Miteirya Ridge, something that Rommel would have been horrified by had he been on the spot. This success was not mirrored during the night by X Corps. Each of its armoured divisions had the responsibility of clearing its own minefield gaps. The clearance teams were to work closely with the infantry to open three gaps for its parent division, each wide enough for tanks. It was planned that these gaps would be completely swept and marked during the hours of darkness, allowing the armoured divisions to exploit southwards from XXX Corps final objectives before dawn. They would then be ready to meet the expected Panzer counterattacks on ground of their own choosing. Unfortunately, this did not happen.

The corps had priority on all forward tracks from 0200hrs. Its clearance teams came forward as planned but then worked in confusing and hazardous conditions to locate and clear mines by hand and with mine detectors. The northern corridor for 1st Armoured Division was located close to the junction of the Australian and Highland Divisions. Results that night were mixed with one marked gap actually completed through as far as the forward infantry, but the others slowed down by pockets of enemy resistance close to their routes. The other gap for 10th Armoured Division was located in the New Zealand sector further south. Here there was a little more success with four routes marked right up to the Miteirya Ridge, although only one was actually usable at the western end. Immense traffic jams at the eastern end of all the routes prevented many tanks getting through to the forward edge of the penetration. Those that did were met with heavy anti-tank fire from many parts of the enemy main defences that were still intact. By dawn his fire forced those tanks that had made it onto the ridge back over the crest to hull-down positions in the rear. In some cases the armour made a complete withdrawal right back off the ridge. When daylight came, neither 1st nor 10th Armoured Divisions were in a position to exploit XXX Corps' penetration.

Down in the south, Horrocks' XIII Corps had put in its attack the previous night in concert with those in the north. MajGen Harding's 7th Armoured Division met the same resistance and difficulties when trying to penetrate the minefields as had the divisions of XXX and X Corps. The division's right flank was protected by an attack by 131st Brigade of 44th Division which ran into difficulties soon after the start. Only the first of two large enemy minefields was actually penetrated by XIII Corps before dawn, but the attack helped confuse the enemy in the southern sector of the line as did BrigGen Koenig's diversionary moves against Qaret el Himeimat and Naqb Rala with his Free French Brigade.

When details began to filter into Montgomery's HQ early in the morning, he was rather pleased with the preliminary results. The attacks had gone reasonably well, although X Corps did not have as many tanks forward through the minefields as hoped. Enemy resistance had been fierce as had been expected, but progress had been made all along the line. If the bridgehead could be strengthened as planned, crumbling attacks could begin to grind down Axis infantry and provoke a showdown with the Panzer divisions. The outcome of the battle would then depend on who could best endure the battle of attrition that would follow.

Enemy casualties and kit lie scattered around a fortified position that had been overrun during Operation *Lightfoot*. These positions were difficult to see and to locate in the featureless desert, often remaining undetected by the advancing infantry until machine-gun fire ripped their ranks. (IWM E18657)

EL ALAMEIN: THE DOG FIGHT

Dawn on 24 October brought with it a fair degree of optimism regarding the results of the previous night, but daylight also introduced new problems for Montgomery's forces. During the morning all formations were trying to get their vehicles into the bridgehead that had been carved through the enemy minefields. Smoke, dust, shell fire and mines all helped to create a fog of battle that introduced an element of chaos into the proceedings. Six divisions from two corps were all attempting to clear gaps for their own use in an area that had no fixed boundaries or recognizable features, whilst all the while being harassed by an enemy who had not yet been fully evicted. It is not surprising then that traffic jams and frayed tempers began to influence decisions.

LtGen Montgomery intended to continue with the plan he had laid out before the battle. Work was to resume carving out the corridors on XXX Corps front. The 51st Division was to push on to its primary objective and help clear 1st Armoured Division's gaps. New Zealand Division was to get onto the Miteirya Ridge then exploit southwards. MajGen Gatehouse's 10th Armoured Division was ordered to advance with strong artillery support over the ridge to protect the New Zealanders' flank. Montgomery told LtGen Lumsden that he was prepared to accept casualties amongst his corps, but he had to get the tanks forward. On the extreme right flank the Australian Division would begin its crumbling operations northwards starting that night, the South Africans would do likewise on the other flank. In the far south, Horrocks was told that if 7th Armoured Division could not get through the second minefield, then 44th Division would have to force a gap with a night attack. Maximum air effort in support of ground forces that day was requested from AVM. Coningham and his aircraft rose to the occasion by flying over 1,000 sorties.

On the enemy side there was something approaching dismay. The attack had achieved complete surprise and for almost an hour after the assault had begun there was little response from the Axis artillery. The effects of British artillery, and the jamming of German radio frequencies, had disrupted Axis communications and resulted in most news of the attacks having to be relayed by messengers to senior commanders. It took time before an overall appreciation of the offensive could be built up at Panzerarmee HQ. The simultaneous attacks on the line from the sea to the Qattara Depression meant that its commander, Gen d.Kav Stumme, was unable to determine which thrust was the main one. He had surmised that the main British effort would be delivered just south of the centre, but no reports could confirm that this had in fact happened. Desperate to assess matters, Stumme set out for the front to see for himself. It was a mistake, for as he neared the sector of the line opposite

LtGen Montgomery with two of his armoured commanders. From left to right: Brig 'Pip' Roberts (22nd Armoured Brigade), Montgomery and MajGen Gatehouse (10th Armoured Division). (IWM E16484)

the Australians his staff car was shelled and he died of a heart attack. The loss of Stumme at this most critical time in the battle was a huge blow to the enemy.

For a while no one knew what had happened to Stumme, or where he was. By midday the awful realization that Panzerarmee Afrika was leaderless became apparent and command passed temporarily to Gen d.Pz von Thoma. He had no better idea of the true situation than had Stumme and decided to contain the British attacks locally rather than commit any of the armoured formations. In Berlin the crisis was also viewed with alarm at OKW. At around 1500hrs a message was sent to Rommel. He was summoned from his convalescence and ordered to return to Africa and take over the battle. He arrived late the following day.

Crew of a Crusader tank cook breakfast beside their tank in the early October morning sunshine. (IWM R16266)

Progress made by Eighth Army on 24 October was disappointing. Few tanks made it completely through the minefields in either of the armour's corridors. Only minor gains were made by 51st Division. The Highlanders put in an attack to clear a passage for MajGen Briggs' 1st Armoured Division in the afternoon, but although some tanks of 2nd Armoured Brigade got beyond the German obstacles, they remained well short of their objective, Kidney Ridge. Montgomery continued to urge his armoured commanders to get their divisions through the minefields and out into the open where they could manoeuvre, but little effort was made to comply with the order. LtGen Freyberg was incensed with MajGen Gatehouse's unwillingness to exploit the success of his infantry. The commander of 10th Armoured Division said that his tanks would be shot to pieces if they ventured over the ridge and he seemed preoccupied with getting his division into position to repel an enemy attack rather than to initiate one of his own. Further urging and pleading by Leese not to let the opportunity slip by, also failed to get the armoured divisions moving.

After a meeting with his commanders, Lumsden signalled Montgomery that his corps would attack that night. Montgomery signalled back that they must attack that afternoon. To comply with the army commander's wishes, Gatehouse's 8th Armoured Brigade sent a reconnaissance attack across the Miteirya Ridge at 1600hrs that afternoon only to find a new minefield covered by anti-tank guns. The half-hearted advance stopped three hours later when Lumsden signalled to his chief that the attack would resume later that night.

That night's operations by 10th Armoured Division had massive artillery support from the guns of the division and those of 51st and 2nd New Zealand Divisions. After a period of counter-battery fire and a heavy barrage, Gatehouse's two armoured brigades, the 8th and 24th, intended to advance over the top of the ridge supported by 133rd Lorried Infantry Brigade. When the attack got underway it immediately got caught up in the minefield along the crest of the Miteirya Ridge. Enemy shellfire hampered attempts to clear gaps and then the Luftwaffe put in an air attack on the waiting armour. The raid caused some disorganization as the armour dispersed for safety. When the attack tried to resume the artillery barrage had gone too far forward for the tanks to catch up with

British infantry on a daylight patrol near enemy lines. The flat open terrain of the desert made this a particularly hazardous task. (IWM E14582)

it and Brig Custance, commander 24th Brigade, advised the divisional commander that it was inadvisable to go on with the advance. Gatehouse agreed, fearful that daylight would find the division in some disarray, with tanks still on the forward slope or caught in the minefield. Freyberg was appalled with the decision; he needed armoured protection if his division was to exploit to the south and relayed the news of the delays to his corps commander.

When Leese reported this news to Eighth Army's HQ, the sleeping Montgomery was roused from his bed and became most annoyed at news of the setback. The army commander then met with his two corps commanders at his Tactical HQ at 0330hrs and told them both that 10th Armoured would break out that night as ordered. Monty also told Lumsden that he would have no hesitation in removing commanders if his orders were not carried out. This blunt speaking seemed to have some effect, for during the night news began to filter back that 24th Brigade had broken through into the open and was in contact with 2nd Armoured Brigade on its right. Ninth Armoured Brigade had also got through the minefield and was ready to support the New Zealanders in their crumbling operations the next day. LtGen Montgomery went back to bed thinking that his armour was at last out in the open ready to challenge the Panzer divisions and attack them.

The next morning it was soon realized that none of this had in fact happened and there was no armour whatsoever on the forward slopes of the Miteirya Ridge. The 1st Armoured Division also did not have 2nd Armoured Brigade on Kidney Ridge. To make matters worse, Horrocks had called off the attack by 7th Armoured Division in the south, citing problems in getting through the minefields.

In view of these failures, LtGen Freyberg reported that his division could not now start the crumbling attacks as planned. He had completely lost faith in the British armour and doubted whether Gatehouse would ever get his division to break out beyond the Miteirya Ridge. Freyberg even suggested that the New Zealand Division should put in an artillery supported attack with its own infantry to gain a position 4,000 metres beyond the ridge for Gatehouse's tanks. Monty refused, knowing that the attack would be costly for the infantry. He required these infantry for the crumbling operations that were to follow and was well aware of the high losses already suffered by the troops of three of the four divisions of XXX Corps that had forced their way through the minefields. Only the Australians were anything like near their full strength.

On the other side of the battlefield, Gen von Arnim had been puzzled by British actions since the battle began. The British had taken the advantage during the first night, but had declined to press this advantage the next morning or in the afternoon. This allowed the temporary commander of Panzerarmee to move more guns into the critical Miteirya area and to lay more mines. He predicted that the British would then attack that night, 24 October, with infantry. What in fact came at his forces in the dark was a huge artillery barrage and a half-hearted attack by armour. This convinced von Thoma that the thrust from the Miteirya Ridge was the main British effort and sent some of his tanks into the area to be ready for it.

Operation *Lightfoot* was not going according to plan for Montgomery. Although XXX Corps had almost reached most of its original objectives, the armoured divisions were just not performing. Casualties amongst the infantry, although not excessive, were still high and amounted to over 4,500. There were no reinforcements available for the New Zealand or South African Divisions, and the Highland Division's casualties had reached 2,100. These losses had been suffered even though the enemy had not committed the whole Afrika Korps or 90th Light Division, although some tanks of 15th Panzer Division had been sent against the Miteirya Ridge area. Monty knew that the failure of a night attack by the New Zealand infantry or another refusal to implement his orders by the armoured commanders could result in stalemate, or worse, especially if the Panzer divisions were moved against him before his armoured divisions were in a position to receive them.

MajGen Briggs, Commander 1st Armoured Division (left) with LtGen Lumsden (right). Montgomery was not best pleased with the performance of his armoured commanders during the opening stages of the Alamein battle. (IWM E16464)

He decided to change his original plan. He needed to try to surprise the enemy and retain the initiative. In a bold move he now ordered the right-hand sector of the break-in to carry the main weight of the attack. He intended that the 1st Armoured Division would push forward to form a shield for the Australian Division who would then begin its crumbling operations northwards towards the sea. He hoped that this new line of attack would catch the enemy unawares and threaten to take the coast road. If the attack was successful, he could switch the whole axis of this advance to the north and the enemy would be compelled to move his Panzer divisions against it. In the meantime, 10th Armoured Division would be withdrawn, except for 24th Armoured Brigade which would join 1st Armoured Division. The remainder of XXX Corps would continue to hold the line along the Miteirya Ridge.

On 25 October, 1st Armoured Division attacked north-westwards but made little headway against enemy anti-tank defences. During the day it dealt with an attack by German and Italian armour, beating the enemy back with the loss of 34 of its own tanks. The Australians, meanwhile, continued with their preparations for the attack northwards. In the south, 50th Division attempted and failed to penetrate the enemy minefield on its front and 44th Division took over the ground that 7th Armoured Division had won. The disappointing results gained by XIII Corps did, however, have a wider significance in that its attacks had kept 21st Panzer and Ariete Divisions in the southern sector away from the main effort in the north.

On the night of 25/26 October the 51st Highland Division made ground towards its original objective line on 'Oxalic'. At the same time, a little further north, LtGen Morshead's 9th Australian Division attacked towards the strategically important ground at Point 29. This slight rise

Soft sand makes all movement difficult for this artillery quad towing its 25-Pounder field gun. When forward movement bogs down, it is a case of everyone out and push. (IWM E14037)

gave good observation over the northern section of the battlefield with exceptionally good sight towards the coast. The assault was put in by 26th Australian Brigade supported by the Valentine tanks of 40th RTR and the guns of five field and two medium regiments of artillery. In the air 79 sorties were flown by Wellingtons and Albacores which dropped 115 tons of bombs on targets in the battle area. German fighters were kept at bay by night-flying Hurricanes. The Australian attack was a complete success and well before dawn the 26th Brigade had two battalions dug in on the feature ready to deal with any enemy counterattack.

GFM Rommel had arrived back at Panzerarmee's HQ the previous evening. He was shocked by what had happened since his departure and with the reports that were given to him regarding fuel and supplies. Little of what had been promised had been delivered. The lack of fuel worried him most, for the shortages restricted the mobility of his army just when he needed speed and manoeuvrability. When news arrived of the loss of Point 29, he ordered an immediate counterattack by elements of 15th Panzer and 164th Divisions, together with infantry and tanks from Italian XX Corps. He was concerned that this British success would be followed up by an armoured thrust north-west towards the coast road.

Rommel's counterattack was unsuccessful. His assembled forces were strafed and bombed the whole day and British and Australian Artillery broke up his formations as they approached Point 29, forcing the move to be abandoned. Later that day Rommel decided to move his reserve forward and brought 90th Light Division eastwards in front of Point 29. He also contemplated bringing 21st Panzer and Ariete Divisions north to reinforce the sector, but knew that if he did so he would not have enough fuel to move them back again.

The enemy reaction to the moves by the Australians had strengthened Montgomery's hand. Rommel was beginning to engage more and more of his tanks in countering each of the small gains made by Eighth Army. The fighting all along the front was grinding down Rommel's forces and eating away at his strength. Although Montgomery didn't fully realize it, the sheer size of the British attack was forcing Rommel to spend his force in penny packets. The field marshal's

THE DOG FIGHT

After Operation *Lightfoot* had broken into the German line, as far as Phase Line *Oxalic*, Gen Montgomery knew that he would have to engage the Axis armoured divisions in a 'dog fight' to draw off some of their strength prior to launching his breakout offensive, Operation *Supercharge*.

Note: Gridlines are shown at intervals of 2 miles

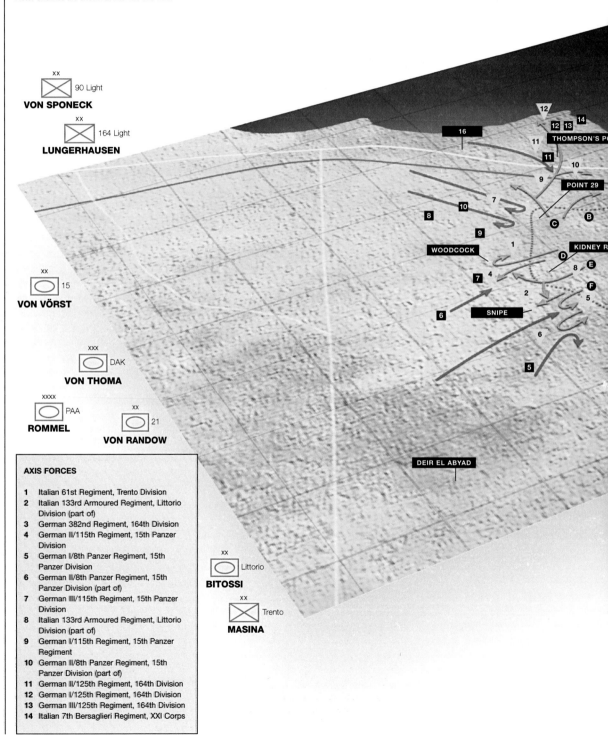

VON SPONECK — XX 90 Light

LUNGERHAUSEN — XX 164 Light

VON VÖRST — XX 15

VON THOMA — XXX DAK

ROMMEL — XXXX PAA

VON RANDOW — XX 21

BITOSSI — XX Littorio

MASINA — XX Trento

16   11   12   13   14   12   THOMPSON'S P(
11   10
9   POINT 29
7
8   10   C   B
9   KIDNEY R
WOODCOCK   1   D   8   E
7   4   F
2   5
6   SNIPE
6
5
DEIR EL ABYAD

AXIS FORCES

1   Italian 61st Regiment, Trento Division
2   Italian 133rd Armoured Regiment, Littorio Division (part of)
3   German 382nd Regiment, 164th Division
4   German II/115th Regiment, 15th Panzer Division
5   German I/8th Panzer Regiment, 15th Panzer Division
6   German II/8th Panzer Regiment, 15th Panzer Division (part of)
7   German III/115th Regiment, 15th Panzer Division
8   Italian 133rd Armoured Regiment, Littorio Division (part of)
9   German I/115th Regiment, 15th Panzer Regiment
10   German II/8th Panzer Regiment, 15th Panzer Division (part of)
11   German II/125th Regiment, 164th Division
12   German I/125th Regiment, 164th Division
13   German III/125th Regiment, 164th Division
14   Italian 7th Bersaglieri Regiment, XXI Corps

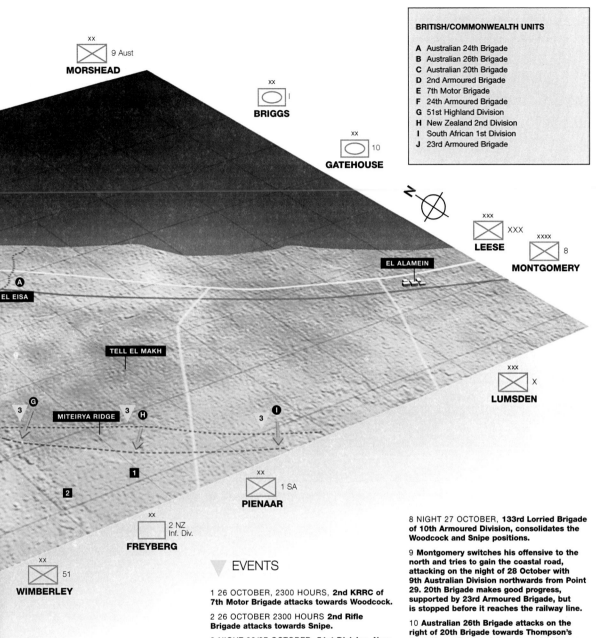

BRITISH/COMMONWEALTH UNITS

A Australian 24th Brigade
B Australian 26th Brigade
C Australian 20th Brigade
D 2nd Armoured Brigade
E 7th Motor Brigade
F 24th Armoured Brigade
G 51st Highland Division
H New Zealand 2nd Division
I South African 1st Division
J 23rd Armoured Brigade

MORSHEAD
9 Aust

BRIGGS
I

GATEHOUSE
10

EL ALAMEIN

LEESE
XXX

MONTGOMERY
8

EL EISA
A

TELL EL MAKH

LUMSDEN
X

MITEIRYA RIDGE
G 3 3 H 3 I

1

2

PIENAAR
1 SA

FREYBERG
2 NZ
Inf. Div.

WIMBERLEY
51

▼ EVENTS

1 26 OCTOBER, 2300 HOURS, **2nd KRRC of 7th Motor Brigade attacks towards Woodcock.**

2 26 OCTOBER 2300 HOURS **2nd Rifle Brigade attacks towards Snipe.**

3 NIGHT 26/27 OCTOBER, **51st Division, New Zealand 2nd Division and South African 1st Division attack to extend the front southwards to conform with** *Lightfoot*'s **first objectives.**

4 27 OCTOBER, **2nd Armoured Brigade advances to pass round 2nd KRRC but is stopped by counter attack by 15th Panzer Division.**

5 27 OCTOBER, **24th Armoured Brigade attacks to the south of Snipe, but meets 8th Panzer Regiment.**

6 **21st Panzer Division and I/8th Panzer Regiment counter attack during the afternoon of 27 October, but fail to push back the British.**

7 **90th Light Division and 12th Bersaglieri Regiment attack Point 29 late afternoon of 27 October, but are repulsed by Australian 9th Division.**

8 NIGHT 27 OCTOBER, **133rd Lorried Brigade of 10th Armoured Division, consolidates the Woodcock and Snipe positions.**

9 **Montgomery switches his offensive to the north and tries to gain the coastal road, attacking on the night of 28 October with 9th Australian Division northwards from Point 29. 20th Brigade makes good progress, supported by 23rd Armoured Brigade, but is stopped before it reaches the railway line.**

10 **Australian 26th Brigade attacks on the right of 20th Brigade towards Thompson's Post. Heavy fighting follows in which German I/125th Regiment is virtually destroyed.**

11 **The two Australian attacks cause Rommel to switch some of his forces to the north on 29 October. German 90th Light Division is moved against the Australians to stop them gaining the coast road. Heavy fighting draws more German units into the area when elements of 21st Panzer Division join in the struggle.**

12 **A fresh attack by Australian 26th Brigade on night of 30 October clashes again with 90th Light Division, but manages to cross the railway line and coastal road to reach the sea. Rommel is certain that this attack will be followed by Eighth Army's main breakout battle in this sector, but Montgomery has by then decided to launch his Operation** *Supercharge* **further south near Woodcock and Snipe.**

strength was diminishing to a point where it was in danger of becoming critical. Fifteenth Panzer Division for instance was down to just 40 tanks.

Montgomery now decided that the Australians should renew their attack northwards again on the night of the 28th/29th. Before that, 1st Armoured Division would put in another attack against the area around Kidney Ridge with 7th Motor and 2nd Armoured Brigades, while 51st, New Zealand and South African Divisions cleared any of the enemy still holding out in their sectors and advanced to the original Oxalic line wherever they were short of it. Monty also decided to create a reserve ready to launch against the enemy at a time suitable for exploitation. XXX Corps was told to withdraw the New Zealand Division and 9th Armoured Brigade on 27 and 28 October to join 10th Armoured Division in this reserve and to hold its sector of the line by redistributing other formations within the corps. The 7th Armoured Division was also given warning of a move north to join the reserve.

While these moves were being organized, 1st Armoured Division began an advance from the northern corridor to draw onto itself some of the enemy armour and to help the Australians on its right. On the night of 26 October, 7th Motor Brigade made an attack against two centres of resistance either side of Kidney Ridge – 'Woodstock' in the north and 'Snipe' in the south – both located approximately 1.5 kilometres from the ridge itself. Woodstock became the objective of 2nd Kings Royal Rifle Corps; Snipe was the goal of 2nd Rifle Brigade. These night attacks were required to seize these locations before dawn to allow 2nd Armoured Brigade to pass around to the north and 24th Armoured Brigade to advance to the south.

The attack got underway as planned at 2300hrs on 26 October behind a barrage fired by all the guns of both X and XXX Corps. Both battalions of 7th Motor Brigade made a successful advance and established themselves on or near their objectives, although they found that the featureless terrain made it difficult to pinpoint their locations exactly. At around 0600hrs the 2nd and 24th Armoured Brigades began their advance. Their progress was slow in the face of increasing enemy resistance, but by midday both were close to the battalions of 7th Motor Brigade. The moves had attracted opposition from the Littorio Division and from elements of both of the German Panzer Divisions. During the day each side pounded the other continuously as the British tanks

attempted to gain a breakthrough. Rommel, in turn, recognized the growing danger of the British moves and was determined to push back the British away from his main defence line. He ordered an immediate attack against the Kidney Ridge area.

In the afternoon the situation facing 1st Armoured Division deteriorated rapidly as all three brigades suddenly found themselves dealing with a full-scale German armoured counterattack. Rommel's blow fell most heavily on the Snipe area and was met by the 6-pdr anti-tank guns of 2nd Rifle Brigade and 239th Anti-tank Battery RA. The defence put up by these units was brave and dogged. The battalion, in the words of the official history, 'stood its ground and did great execution, particularly amongst enemy tanks advancing against 24th Armoured Brigade'. More than once it seemed that the battalion would be wiped out, but it hung on defiantly. The heroic stand made by the 2nd Rifle Brigade defeated the enemy counterattack completely; the enemy could not endure the losses taken by his tanks and withdrew. The 2nd Rifle Brigade's commander, LtCol V. B. Turner, fully deserved the Victoria Cross awarded to him for the action. Axis attacks against Point 29 by German 90th Light Division also failed that day.

That night 133rd Lorried Brigade came forward to help hold on to the gains and deal with further small counterattacks against the positions. The next day the pressure on the enemy continued when Montgomery shifted his weight northwards and launched 9th Australian Division towards the coastal road. This new push opened on the night of 28 October with 20th Australian Brigade making a set-piece attack to enlarge the ground already taken around Point 29. A simultaneous assault by 26th Australian Brigade on the right striking northwards towards the railway line and the coastal road hoped to widen this penetration. Good progress was initially made in these attacks, but increasing enemy resistance stopped them both before they could reach their objectives. None the less, the attacks were deemed to be a success for they caused great destruction to the units of German 164th and 90th Divisions pitted

OPERATION SUPERCHARGE: THE BREAK OUT

Launched in the early hours of 2 November, Operation *Supercharge* was designed to penetrate Rommel's main line south of the salient formed by 9th Australian Division. Montgomery intended to use the reinforced New Zealand Division to punch a hole through the Axis positions, hold open the breach with 9th Armoured Brigade and allow X Corps to pass through.

Note: Gridlines are shown at intervals of 2 miles

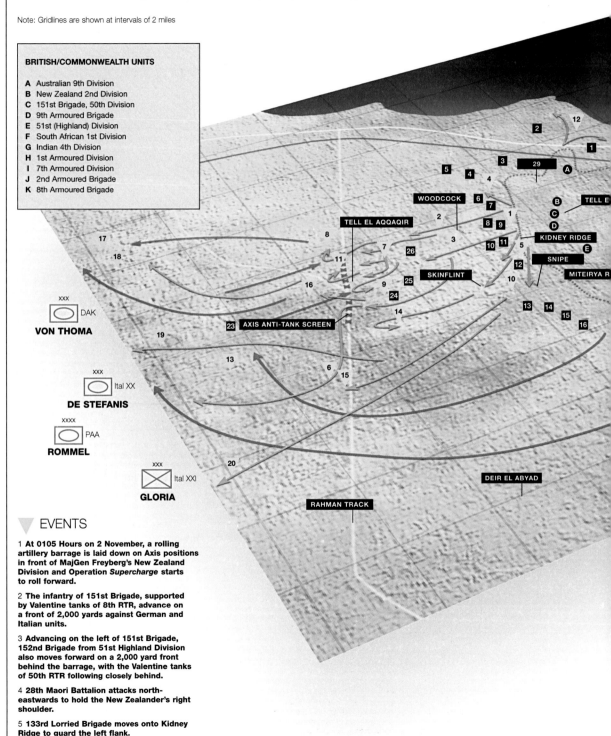

BRITISH/COMMONWEALTH UNITS

A Australian 9th Division
B New Zealand 2nd Division
C 151st Brigade, 50th Division
D 9th Armoured Brigade
E 51st (Highland) Division
F South African 1st Division
G Indian 4th Division
H 1st Armoured Division
I 7th Armoured Division
J 2nd Armoured Brigade
K 8th Armoured Brigade

▼ EVENTS

1 **At 0105 Hours on 2 November, a rolling artillery barrage is laid down on Axis positions in front of MajGen Freyberg's New Zealand Division and Operation *Supercharge* starts to roll forward.**

2 **The infantry of 151st Brigade, supported by Valentine tanks of 8th RTR, advance on a front of 2,000 yards against German and Italian units.**

3 **Advancing on the left of 151st Brigade, 152nd Brigade from 51st Highland Division also moves forward on a 2,000 yard front behind the barrage, with the Valentine tanks of 50th RTR following closely behind.**

4 **28th Maori Battalion attacks north-eastwards to hold the New Zealander's right shoulder.**

5 **133rd Lorried Brigade moves onto Kidney Ridge to guard the left flank.**

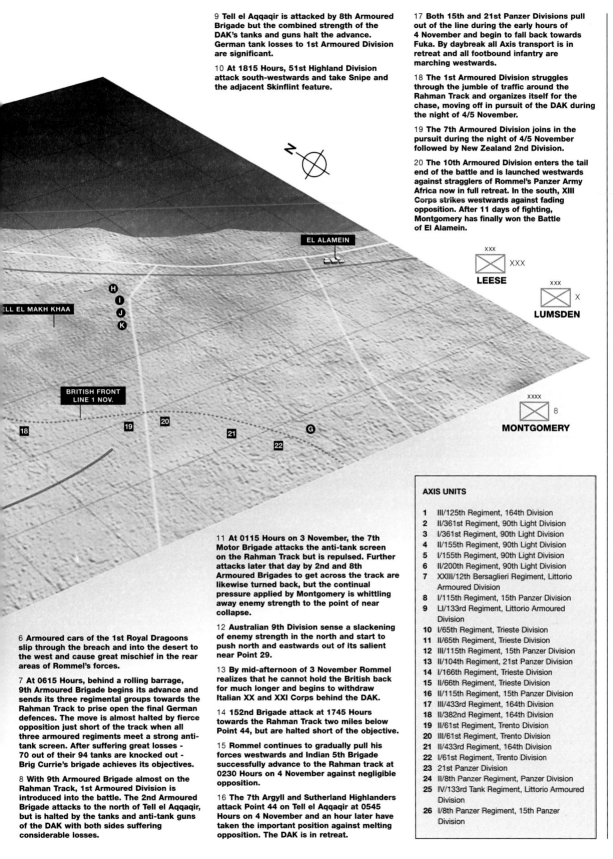

9 **Tell el Aqqaqir is attacked by 8th Armoured Brigade but the combined strength of the DAK's tanks and guns halt the advance. German tank losses to 1st Armoured Division are significant.**

10 **At 1815 Hours, 51st Highland Division attack south-westwards and take Snipe and the adjacent Skinflint feature.**

17 **Both 15th and 21st Panzer Divisions pull out of the line during the early hours of 4 November and begin to fall back towards Fuka. By daybreak all Axis transport is in retreat and all footbound infantry are marching westwards.**

18 **The 1st Armoured Division struggles through the jumble of traffic around the Rahman Track and organizes itself for the chase, moving off in pursuit of the DAK during the night of 4/5 November.**

19 **The 7th Armoured Division joins in the pursuit during the night of 4/5 November followed by New Zealand 2nd Division.**

20 **The 10th Armoured Division enters the tail end of the battle and is launched westwards against stragglers of Rommel's Panzer Army Africa now in full retreat. In the south, XIII Corps strikes westwards against fading opposition. After 11 days of fighting, Montgomery has finally won the Battle of El Alamein.**

EL ALAMEIN

LEESE

LUMSDEN

MONTGOMERY

ELL EL MAKH KHAA

BRITISH FRONT LINE 1 NOV.

11 **At 0115 Hours on 3 November, the 7th Motor Brigade attacks the anti-tank screen on the Rahman Track but is repulsed. Further attacks later that day by 2nd and 8th Armoured Brigades to get across the track are likewise turned back, but the continual pressure applied by Montgomery is whittling away enemy strength to the point of near collapse.**

6 **Armoured cars of the 1st Royal Dragoons slip through the breach and into the desert to the west and cause great mischief in the rear areas of Rommel's forces.**

7 **At 0615 Hours, behind a rolling barrage, 9th Armoured Brigade begins its advance and sends its three regimental groups towards the Rahman Track to prise open the final German defences. The move is almost halted by fierce opposition just short of the track when all three armoured regiments meet a strong anti-tank screen. After suffering great losses - 70 out of their 94 tanks are knocked out - Brig Currie's brigade achieves its objectives.**

8 **With 9th Armoured Brigade almost on the Rahman Track, 1st Armoured Division is introduced into the battle. The 2nd Armoured Brigade attacks to the north of Tell el Aqqaqir, but is halted by the tanks and anti-tank guns of the DAK with both sides suffering considerable losses.**

12 **Australian 9th Division sense a slackening of enemy strength in the north and start to push north and eastwards out of its salient near Point 29.**

13 **By mid-afternoon of 3 November Rommel realizes that he cannot hold the British back for much longer and begins to withdraw Italian XX and XXI Corps behind the DAK.**

14 **152nd Brigade attack at 1745 Hours towards the Rahman Track two miles below Point 44, but are halted short of the objective.**

15 **Rommel continues to gradually pull his forces westwards and Indian 5th Brigade successfully advance to the Rahman track at 0230 Hours on 4 November against negligible opposition.**

16 **The 7th Argyll and Sutherland Highlanders attack Point 44 on Tell el Aqqaqir at 0545 Hours on 4 November and an hour later have taken the important position against melting opposition. The DAK is in retreat.**

AXIS UNITS

1	III/125th Regiment, 164th Division
2	II/361st Regiment, 90th Light Division
3	I/361st Regiment, 90th Light Division
4	II/155th Regiment, 90th Light Division
5	I/155th Regiment, 90th Light Division
6	II/200th Regiment, 90th Light Division
7	XXIII/12th Bersaglieri Regiment, Littorio Armoured Division
8	I/115th Regiment, 15th Panzer Division
9	LI/133rd Regiment, Littorio Armoured Division
10	I/65th Regiment, Trieste Division
11	I/65th Regiment, Trieste Division
12	III/115th Regiment, 15th Panzer Division
13	II/104th Regiment, 21st Panzer Division
14	I/166th Regiment, Trieste Division
15	I/66th Regiment, Trieste Division
16	II/115th Regiment, 15th Panzer Division
17	III/433rd Regiment, 164th Division
18	II/382nd Regiment, 164th Division
19	II/61st Regiment, Trento Division
20	III/61st Regiment, Trento Division
21	II/433rd Regiment, 164th Division
22	I/61st Regiment, Trento Division
23	21st Panzer Division
24	II/8th Panzer Regiment, Panzer Division
25	IV/133rd Tank Regiment, Littorio Armoured Division
26	I/8th Panzer Regiment, 15th Panzer Division

against them. Armour from 15th Panzer Division was also attracted northwards to help stem the attack.

The two Australian attacks caused Rommel to switch more and more of his forces to the north. On 29 October elements of 21st Panzer Division came up from the south and joined in the struggle against the Australians. The fighting in this northern sector led Montgomery to contemplate making his breakthrough here. His divisions were engaged in a dog fight in which his superior strength and resources must prevail. He now decided that he would move the New Zealand Division into the area to maintain the momentum of the infantry attacks, prior to launching his armoured reserve in a breakout battle along the coast road.

A fresh attack by Australian 26th Brigade on the night of 30 October clashed again with 90th Light Division and did great execution. The advance continued across the railway line and coastal road to reach the sea. It then attempted to turn eastwards to capture a defended locality called Thompson's Post, encircling the First Battalion of German 125th Regiment. Although the attacks did not achieve all that was planned, they did form a salient across the road and railway line through which the trapped enemy forces found it difficult to withdraw. These moves made Rommel certain that this attack would be followed by Eighth Army's main breakout attempt through this salient towards Sidi Abd el Rahman and for a brief moment he considered making a general withdrawal to a new line at Fuka. He decided to withdraw 21st Panzer Division to an area north of Point 44 at Tel el Aqqaqir to form a mobile reserve. Rommel knew that he would need this reserve to counter any possible breakthrough in the north. More bad news arrived at his HQ that day when he heard that the tanker *Luisiano* had been sunk and little more fuel would reach his army in the near future.

Rommel had read Montgomery's thoughts correctly when he predicted that the British might try to break through in the north, but by then Eighth Army's commander had changed his mind again. The main effort would now go through south of this sector. Montgomery had formulated a new plan for his great breakout battle, one which, in his words, 'would hit Rommel for six'.

EL ALAMEIN: BREAKOUT AND PURSUIT

LtGen Montgomery's new plan for the breakout was called *Supercharge* and was similar in concept to *Lightfoot*. XXX Corps' infantry would attack in strength at night followed closely by the armour. Simultaneously, in the south, Horrocks' depleted XIII Corps would lead the enemy into thinking that an attack was going in there. The location and direction of *Supercharge* would be out of a 4,000-metre front just to the south of the Australian-held ground around Point 29. As before there would be tremendous support from both artillery and the aircraft of the Desert Air Force. There was one added advantage in that there would be no deep minefields to contend with during the initial attack. Mines would be present, but only in scattered patches. This time, Montgomery insisted, armour would be passed through the infantry without any loss of momentum.

The New Zealand Division would carry out the initial infantry attack, strengthened by the addition of several other formations. It would make the assault with 151st Brigade from 50th Division and 152nd Brigade from 51st Division under command, both with a battalion of tanks in support. Following closely behind would be 9th Armoured Brigade, also under LtGen Freyberg's command. This brigade would carry the attack from the infantry's objective for another two kilometres behind a rolling barrage to smash through and capture the enemy defences around the Rahman track. The momentum would then be taken up by 1st Armoured Division who would take on the Panzer divisions backed by its

Gen Montgomery in a classic pose standing in the turret of his Grant tank. With his black beret on his head and binoculars in hand this was the image flashed around the world during his moment of victory. (IWM E18980)

THE ACTION FOUGHT BY THE 3RD KING'S OWN HUSSARS NEAR THE RAHMAN TRACK ON 2 NOVEMBER DURING OPERATION *SUPERCHARGE* (pages 84–85)

Montgomery's final battle to break through Rommel's positions at Alamein, Operation *Supercharge*, began late on 1 November with an attack by the reinforced New Zealand Division. At 0615 Hours the next day, behind a rolling barrage, 9th Armoured Brigade took up the advance with orders to break through the enemy anti-tank and field-gun positions to 'hold the door open' for the 1st Armoured Division of X Corps. Montgomery told the commander, Brig Currie, that he was prepared to take 100 per cent casualties in order for the brigade to reach the Rahman track. When the CO of The 3rd The King's Own Hussars, Lt Col Sir Peter Farquhar, protested that 'this was just suicide,' Montgomery remained adamant. The advance by the 3rd King's Own Hussars is recognized as one of the greatest armoured regimental actions of the war. The Hussars faced fierce enemy opposition and shellfire during the whole of the operation. On the move up to the start line alone, it lost most of its carriers and soft-skinned vehicles to shell fire. By the time it had arrived on the infantry objective ready to begin its own attack, ten of its tanks had been destroyed. The Hussars battled their way forward and eventually reached the Rahman Track at first light. Unfortunately, at this critical time, the tanks became silhouetted against the dawn sky and drew heavy anti-tank fire. The Hussars pressed on relentlessly through this

barrage, driving straight at the German gun positions, crushing the enemy weapons beneath their tracks. At very close quarters, the tanks were fought to a standstill, having to eliminate each anti-tank gun in turn whilst the Germans returned this fire at point blank range. Soon the battlefield was a mass of burning armour and broken guns, with the Hussars left with just seven serviceable tanks out of the 35 that had set off earlier that morning. But the regiment had gained its objective and broken through the Axis anti-tank line along the Rahman Track just as they had been ordered to do, allowing X Corps a route through the German defences. It was the turning point of Operation *Supercharge*. The battlescene shows the 3rd King's Own Hussars at the height of the action when their tanks had closed right up to the enemy anti-tank gun positions. By this time in the Alamein battle the Hussars had received some of the newly arrived Sherman tanks (1) and were using them to good effect. The mainstay of the regiment were the sturdy Grants (2) and their 75mm and 37mm weapons were particularly useful in this close combat. Also present in the action were the near-obsolete Crusaders (3), but their speed counted for little in this type of battle and most quickly became casualties. The enemy PAK 38 5cm anti-tank gun (4) was one of the enemy's most useful and reliable weapons and did sterling service for the German Army throughout the war. Close by is a burning Panzer II (5), a tank totally outclassed on the battlefield, but still useful as a reconnaissance and close-support weapon for the field guns. (Howard Gerrard)

A British Crusader passes a brewed-up Panzer IV at the end of the battle. (IWM E6751)

anti-tank guns. Either side of this main attack, other divisions would simultaneously whittle away at the Axis defences, probing for an opening through which to exploit.

At 0105hrs on 2 November, Operation *Supercharge* got underway behind an artillery barrage laid down on Axis positions. Prior to this, starting at 2115hrs the previous evening, AVM Coningham's aircraft had begun seven hours of attacks on enemy locations along their line. The Royal Navy also played a part in the operation by simulating landings along the coast, dropping rafts and flares from torpedo boats and filling the air with tracer fire and noise.

The infantry of 151st Brigade, supported by Valentine tanks of 8th RTR, began its advance on a front of 2,000 metres against German and Italian defences. Advancing on their right, 152nd Brigade also moved out behind a rolling barrage, with the Valentine tanks of 50th RTR following closely behind. On the right of these attacks, New Zealand 28th Maori Battalion attacked north-eastwards to hold the northern shoulder of the assault. To the south, the 133rd Lorried Brigade carried out the same defensive task around Kidney Ridge.

The ground attack started well, with both brigades advancing through 4,000 metres of enemy defences to reach their objectives without excessive loss. Taking immediate advantage of the advance, two armoured car regiments tried to slip through the breach out into open country. One, 1st Royal Dragoons, was especially successful and two of its squadrons got out into the desert to the west and caused great mischief in the rear areas of Rommel's forces.

At 0615hrs, behind a rolling barrage, 9th Armoured Brigade split into three groups and took over the advance towards the Rahman Track, aiming to prise open the final German defences. Montgomery had told 9th Brigade's commander, Brig Currie, that he was prepared to take 100 per cent casualties, but the brigade had to get onto the Rahman track. The brigade rose to this challenge and, although almost halted by fierce opposition and a strong anti-tank screen in front of the track, reached

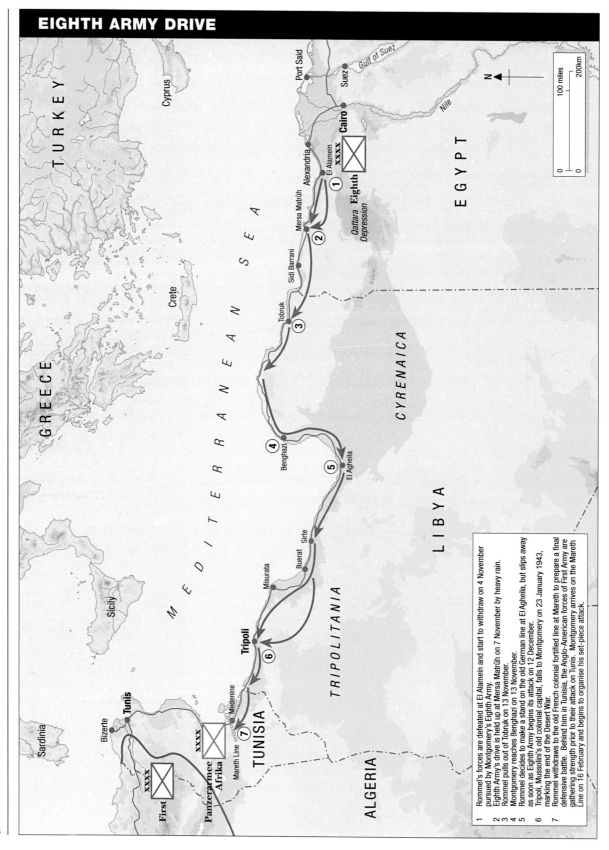

1 Rommel's forces are defeated at El Alamein and start to withdraw on 4 November pursued by Montgomery's Eighth Army.
2 Eighth Army's drive is held up at Mersa Matrûh on 7 November by heavy rain.
3 Rommel pulls out of Tobruk on 13 November.
4 Montgomery reaches Benghazi on 13 November.
5 Rommel decides to make a stand on the old German line at El Agheila, but slips away as soon as Eighth Army begins its attack on 12 December.
6 Tripoli, Mussolini's old colonial capital, falls to Montgomery on 23 January 1943, marking the end of the Desert War.
7 Rommel withdraws to the old French colonial fortified line at Mareth to prepare a final defensive battle. Behind him in Tunisia, the Anglo–American forces of First Army are gathering strength prior to their attack on Tunis. Montgomery arrives on the Mareth Line on 16 February and begins to organise his set-piece attack.

German and Italian prisoners of war are escorted into captivity. When Rommel's forces collapsed at the end of the battle, most of those troops who got away had their own transport. Those infantry who had no access to vehicles, and this included the bulk of the Italian infantry divisions, had to try to make their escape on foot. Thousands of them were captured. (IWM E18485)

its objectives. Losses were substantial – 70 out of their 94 tanks were knocked out – but the dash of Brig Currie's brigade cracked open the enemy line in what has since been recognized as one of the greatest cavalry achievements of the war.

With 9th Armoured Brigade on the Rahman Track, 1st Armoured Division came forward to be introduced into the battle. The 2nd Armoured Brigade attacked to the north of Tel El Aqqaqir, but was halted by the tanks and anti-tank guns of the Afrika Korps with both sides suffering considerable losses. The defences on Point 44 at Tel El Aqqaqir were then attacked by 8th Armoured Brigade which had been transferred to the division for the battle from 10th Armoured Division. The combined strength of the enemy tanks and guns proved to be enough to halt this advance as well, but the Panzer Korps suffered significant losses.

Elsewhere the Axis line was beginning to buckle. Later in the day at 1815 hrs, 51st Highland Division advanced south-westwards to take *Snipe* and the adjacent *Skinflint* feature. Fighting continued through the night. At 0115 hrs on 3rd November, the 7th Motor Brigade attacked the anti-tank screen on the Rahman Track, but was repulsed. Further attacks later that day by 2nd and 8th Armoured Brigades to get across the track were likewise turned back, but the continual pressure applied by Montgomery was whittling away enemy strength to the point of near collapse.

To the north, Australian 9th Division sensed a slackening of enemy resistance and started to push north and eastwards out of its salient near Point 29. By mid-afternoon of 3 November, Rommel realized that he could not hold the British back for much longer and took the heavy decision to begin to withdraw Italian XX and XXI Corps behind the Afrika Korps, but still the British attacks came at him. When Hitler learned of the withdrawals he was furious and ordered Rommel to stand firm. No retreat by any formation was permitted. Rommel reversed his order and prepared for his forces to meet their *Valhalla*. The pressure continued when the 152nd Brigade tried a new assault at 1715hrs towards the Rahman track, three kilometres below Point 44. Rommel's forces halted it just short of its objective.

Axis resistance to the British moves two days into the operation was still dogged, but Montgomery knew that the battle of attrition was swinging in his favour. The enemy was pulling back, but he still did not realize that Rommel's army was so close to the point of collapse. Indian 5th Brigade was now brought northwards to join in the battle and successfully advanced to the Rahman track at 0230hrs on 4 November against negligible opposition. A little later the 7th Argyll and Sutherland Highlanders attacked Point 44 on Tel El Aqqaqir at 0545hrs and an hour later took the strategically important position against melting opposition. Rommel knew that he was beaten. Urgings from Hitler had little effect on his army's resolve, his formations were gradually recoiling westwards; Panzerarmee Afrika was in retreat. Both 15th and 21st Panzer Divisions pulled out of the line during the early hours of 4 November and began to stream back towards Fuka. By daybreak all Axis transport was in full retreat and all footbound infantry that managed to disengage themselves from the fighting were marching westwards.

Montgomery decided that it was now time to unleash his mobile forces. The 1st Armoured Division struggled through the jumble of traffic around the Rahman track and organized itself for the chase, moving off in pursuit of the Afrika Korps on the night of 4/5 November. Then 7th Armoured Division joined in the pursuit during the night followed by New Zealand 2nd Division at first light. Eighth Army Commander then decided that MajGen Gatehouse's 10th Armoured Division could now enter the tail end of the battle and he launched it westwards against the stragglers of Rommel's army now in full flight. In the south XIII Corps was striking out into the desert against fading opposition. After eleven days of fighting, and the loss of 13,560 men killed, wounded and missing, Montgomery had won the Battle of El Alamein.

A great victory had been achieved at El Alamein, but the pursuit of Rommel's beaten army was not the great triumph for Eighth Army that it should have been. Disorganized, fragmented, demoralized and short of fuel, Panzerarmee Afrika was ripe for the *coup de grace* and the vastly superior Eighth Army should have delivered it. For many reasons, some complex and real, others fanciful and apologetic, Montgomery allowed Rommel's forces to slip away along the coast of North Africa. By 13 November Rommel was at Tobruk and a week later in Benghazi. The further west the Axis forces travelled the shorter their supply lines became. The withdrawal was not a rout, but it was a full retreat. There was no longer any hope that Panzerarmee Afrika would ever attain enough strength to go back on to the offensive. Its fate was finally sealed on 8 November when Anglo-American forces landed in Algeria and Morocco and then moved swiftly into Tunisia. Rommel now had an Allied army to his front and rear. The inevitable end of the Desert War came on 13 May 1943 when all those Axis forces that were still fighting on the continent of Africa surrendered to Gen Eisenhower's forces. GFM Erwin Rommel was not among them; the Desert Fox had slipped away to Italy to fight another day.

THE BATTLEFIELD TODAY

The open and featureless desert south of the small railway station of El Alamein has changed little in the sixty years since the battles of 1942; it still remains a most desolate region. The same cannot be said for the stretch of coastline from Alexandria to El Alamein. This has become an almost continuous strip of development. El Alamein itself has also changed and is now a small town of around 5,000 people with a port facility for shipping oil nearby. There are also several small hotels and a beach amenity in the neighbourhood. The tiny railway station beloved of war photographers in 1942 as the only place bearing the name of El Alamein has been replaced by a very modern structure a short distance away, although the old single-story building remains *in situ*.

El Alamein is quite accessible for tourists and is located just over 100 kilometres from Alexandria. To cater for visitors who come to see just where one of the most important battles of the Second World War took place, a museum has been built. Here the battle is explained in dioramas, photographic displays and contemporary exhibits. Those visitors more interested in hardware will find relics of the opposing forces also on show, with examples of the tanks and guns that fought in the battle on display around the outside of the building.

There are several difficulties to be encountered for those who wish to leave the roads and get out into the desert to reach the more remote areas of the battlefield. The area of desert to the south of the coastal road and railway line is vast and most inhospitable for the unwary. It is still devoid of people and settlements, empty save for the few locals who

One of the dangers that still mar the Alamein battlefield today. Wind and weather has uncovered this anti-tank mine, but many of the hundreds of thousands that were laid in 1942 still remain buried and make the whole area very dangerous to the unwary. (Robin Neillands)

The old railway station building at El Alamein as it is today. It has been replaced by a more modern structure a short distance away. (Robin Neillands)

criss-cross the area along the ancient tracks that traverse the sands. It is also a very difficult area to get to. This is not the place for tourists in hire cars to go for a drive, for soft ground, deep gullies and shifting sands can trap the uninitiated. There is also considerable danger from the hundreds of thousands of mines that were laid by both sides during the conflict, many of which still remain, untouched and unlocated.

The most suitable way to experience the detail of the battlefield is with one of the reputable battlefield tour companies who organize visits to site. They will make the arrangements, devise a programme, lay on guest speakers, organize guides and arrange suitable transport. All you then have to do is to enjoy the locations and relive the action. These companies usually have great experience in organizing these trips; they have all done it before and will be prepared for any eventuality. Dates, itineraries and costs can be found on their various web pages on the Internet.

As with all battlefields, the most poignant sites of all are the war cemeteries and mausoleums. There are three in the area, one for British and Commonwealth dead, one for the German fallen and one for Italian victims of the fighting. All are, as you would expect, calm peaceful oases in the parched desert. The British cemetery, administered by the Commonwealth War Graves Commission, looks out from Alamein towards the Miteirya Ridge from a position close by the museum. There are over 8,000 burials located here, together with a roll of names of those who have no known grave. Between the stark headstones there is none of the soft grass that is found in European cemeteries, only wind-blown sand. At the top of the cemetery is an impressive shrine made up of a series of cloisters stretching for almost 90 metres.

The Axis dead are commemorated on two separate sites. The 33-metre high Italian monument was built in 1959 and is situated in an area of 1,500 square metres of ground leased out to the Italian government for 99 years. The names of 4,634 soldiers are inscribed on the mausoleum's walls. The German memorial is shaped like a medieval Teutonic castle and stands on a ridge at Tel el Eisa near the sea. In its inner courtyard a tall obelisk supported by four falcons is ringed by memorial plates and mosaic panels listing the names of 4,200 German dead.

93

BIBLIOGRAPHY

Bierman, John & Smith, Colin, *Alamein: War Without Hate*, Viking, London (2002)

Blaxland, Gregory, *The Plain Cook and the Great Showman*, Kimber, London (1977)

Braddock, D. W., *The Campaigns in Egypt and Libya*, Gale & Polden, Aldershot (1964)

Carver, Michael, *Dilemmas of the Desert War*, Batsford, London (1986)

Carver, Michael, *El Alamein*, Batsford, London (1962)

Delaney, John, *Fighting The Desert Fox*, Arms & Armour, London (1998)

Forty, George, *The Armies of Rommel*, Arms & Armour, London (1997)

Gilbert, Adrian (ed), *The IWM Book of the Desert War*, Sidgwick & Jackson, London (1992)

Hamilton, Nigel, *Monty: The Making of a General 1887–1942*, Hamish Hamilton, London (1981)

Horrocks, LtGen Sir Brian, *A Full Life*, Collins, London (1960)

Irving, David, *The Trail of the Fox*, Weidenfeld & Nicolson, London (1977)

Joslen, LtCol H. F., *Orders of Battle: Second World War 1939–1945*, HMSO London (1960)

Kippenberger, MajGen Sir Howard, *Infantry Brigadier*, Oxford University Press, Oxford (1949)

Liddell Hart, B.H. (ed), *The Rommel Papers*, Collins, London (1953)

Lucas, James, *Panzer Army Africa*, Macdonald & Janes, London (1977)

Messenger, Charles, *The Unknown Alamein*, Ian Allen, Shepperton (1982)

Montgomery, Field Marshal The Viscount, *El Alamein to the River Sangro*, Hutchinson, London (1948)

Pimlott, Dr John, *Rommel In his Own Words*, Greenhill, London (1994)

Playfair, MajGen I.S.O., *The Mediterranean and Middle East Volume III,* HMSO, London (1960)

Playfair, MajGen I.S.O., *The Mediterranean and Middle East Volume IV,* HMSO, London (1966)

Quarrie, Bruce, *Afrika Korps*, Patrick Stephens, Cambridge (1975)

Quarrie, Bruce, *Panzers in the Desert*, Patrick Stephens, Cambridge (1978)

Ryder, Rowland, *Oliver Leese*, Hamish Hamilton, London (1987)

Stewart, Adrian, *The Early Battles of Eighth Army*, Leo Cooper, Barnsley (2002)

INDEX

SECRETS
CHURCHILL'S
WAR ROOMS

Published by IWM, Lambeth Road, London SE1 6HZ
iwm.org.uk

ISBN 978-1-912423-14-9

A catalogue record for this book is
available from the British Library.
Printed and bound by Printer Trento Srl

SECRETS OF CHURCHILL'S WAR ROOMS

Jonathan Asbury

CONTENTS

INTRODUCTION

Churchill didn't enjoy using his War Rooms. When enemy bombs began to drop over London, his natural instinct was to head up the nearest staircase rather than down, seeking out a vantage point from which to watch the action. He is known to have slept in his underground bedroom only a handful of times, and it is thought that he may never have eaten in the dining room set aside for his personal use.

Nonetheless, Churchill was immensely proud of his underground complex. He took great pleasure in showing it off to visiting generals and statesmen, and was particularly fond of the Map Room. Here he could often be found watching the results of his decisions playing out on the charts hung around the walls. He even took an active interest in the fabric of the building, ordering the installation of defensive structures to protect it against bomb blasts, and insisting on making regular torch-lit inspections of progress, clambering over traverses and, on one occasion, soaking his shoes in liquid cement.

While those accidental footprints may not have been preserved for posterity, there are many other tell-tale signs of Churchill's presence throughout the rooms. The microphone on his desk conjures up the trenchant words that he broadcast to the nation from here in the dark days of 1940. His insistence on fast, efficient decision-making survives in the 'Action This Day' labels he invented to mark the most urgent documents. The tension he felt during War Cabinet meetings is still visible decades later in the deep scratch marks he gouged in the arms of his chair.

Those scratch marks give evidence to the fact that, like it or not, Churchill spent a good deal of time locked away in the War Rooms – especially in the months immediately after he became Prime Minister in May 1940, when the possibility of

German invasion loomed, the Battle of Britain raged and, in September, the nightly bombing of London began.

War Rooms staff remember how he used to prowl the corridors in the dead of night 'studying things in his mind', pausing every now and then to peer over the shoulder of one of the typists labouring away at a hastily arranged alcove desk. At other times his bulky frame could be found lying across his bed 'looking…not totally proper' as he dictated a speech to his secretary, or his presence would be announced by a bang on the pipes, warning staff to keep down the noise as he grabbed one of his famous afternoon naps. Even when he was thousands of miles away from Whitehall on one of his many overseas trips, staff recall that the atmosphere and culture of the place owed much to Churchill's animating energy.

Indeed, if Churchill is often seen as the embodiment of – and inspiration for – Britain's steadfast wartime resolution and indefatigable spirit, the War Rooms capture the same qualities in bricks and mortar. Both stand testament to one of the key elements in Britain's eventual triumph – the capacity for brilliant improvisation in the face of deadly necessity. Where else but in Churchill's War Rooms, for example, would one of the most secret communication facilities in the world be kept concealed by the simple addition of a lavatory-style lock on the door?

There have been innumerable accounts of Churchill's role in the Second World War, and also some excellent publications looking at the story of the War Rooms, drawing heavily on the painstaking research undertaken by IWM's historians as they set about their extraordinary preservation and restoration of the site. This book, however, was conceived to perform a slightly different role – to weave together the parallel stories of Churchill and his War Rooms, showing when, how and why Britain's bulldog prime minister made use of them, and explaining his continual reliance on the work that was done there. In so doing, it owes an enormous debt to all those many works of history that precede it.

Taking readers behind the glass screens of the modern-day museum, the book picks out objects and views that not only reveal something about the function of the rooms, but also give an insight into what it was like to work there. In that sense, the book is not only about Churchill and his War Rooms, but also about his War Rooms staff – the remarkable men and women, military and civilian, young and old who worked, ate and slept there in pursuit of survival and, ultimately, victory. It is only by drawing on their first-hand experiences – committed to paper in memoirs, letters and diaries, or related to IWM historians in specially recorded interviews – that the secrets of Churchill's War Rooms can truly be revealed. This book is dedicated to them.

1

THE THREAT AND SHOCK OF WAR

July 1936 to May 1940

On 28 July 1936, backbench MP Winston Churchill stood up to address Prime Minister Stanley Baldwin in a private room at the House of Commons. He had called for the meeting himself, concerned that the government was not doing enough to meet the military threat posed by a resurgent Germany – especially from the air. For an hour and a quarter he laid out his position, and towards the end he posed a question:

> Have we organised and created an alternative centre of government if London is thrown into confusion? No doubt there has been some discussion of this on paper, but has anything been done to provide one or two alternative centres of command, with adequate deep-laid telephone connections and wireless, from which the necessary orders can be given by some coherent thinking-mechanism?

He was talking about the creation of a 'War Room', and the fact was that the government had taken no practical steps in that direction at all.

Churchill himself was partly to blame. After the First World War the British government adopted a 'ten-year rule', instructing every department to operate on the assumption that the country would not go to war again for at least a decade. In 1928, when this ten-year period was coming to an end, Churchill was Chancellor of the Exchequer for the Conservative government, tasked with finding ways to save money. He proposed that the ten-year rule be continually reset, so that the possibility of Britain going to war would forever be pushed a decade into the future. This allowed him to curb defence spending, with the result that little was done to prepare for a future war.

The following year, the Conservatives were voted out of office, and by the time they regained power in 1931 Churchill had fallen out of favour with the party leadership – in particular over the question of Indian Home Rule. The government wanted to grant India the status of a dominion; Churchill did not. For the next four years he argued his case stridently in Parliament, becoming further and further estranged from the party. By 1935, when the government's bill was passed with a resounding majority, Churchill was over 60 years old. He was starting to look like yesterday's man.

In January 1933, the Nazi Party's Adolf Hitler came to power in Germany. In October that year he shocked the world by announcing his country's withdrawal from the League of Nations. His stated reason was simple: it was no longer acceptable for the Western powers to stop Germany from gaining military parity. Germany was set on rearming itself. The chances of war in the next decade were suddenly much higher.

Baldwin decided that the best way to ensure peace was for all sides to commit to disarmament. Churchill, on the other hand, called for Britain to build up its armed forces – not because he would welcome a war, but because he thought that military strength could act as a deterrent as well as an insurance policy.

It was a campaign that he conducted with customary vigour, and which did nothing to reconcile him to the government or to the wider public, who had little appetite for a new war with Germany. 'Germany is arming – she is rapidly arming – and no-one will stop her,' he called out from the back benches, but he was dismissed as 'alarmist' by Prime Minister and newspapers alike.

Several months after Churchill's meeting with Baldwin, the government still had no firm plan from where it would run the next war in the event of a German air attack. As Churchill had suspected, there had been plenty of discussion on paper – one suggestion was for key personnel to be evacuated to the suburbs or out into the West Country – but there had been little or no action.

The idea of a 'war room' in itself was not a new one; it had long been assumed, for example, that each of the three armed services would have one of its own. But what Churchill was asking was how the work of the armed services would be co-ordinated, and crucially how the connection between the government and its fighting forces could be protected.

The dangers of the status quo were revealed in late 1937 when air defence exercises highlighted all sorts of confusion between the armed services. Now, at last, there was talk of a 'combined war room' to house the heads of the Army, Navy and Air Force (known as the Chiefs of Staff), the Deputy Chiefs of Staff and the Joint Planners, whose job it was to assess the military situation and devise suitable strategies.

In response to a request from the Deputy Chiefs, staff at the Air Ministry drew up an elaborate plan for a fully protected, purpose-built underground war room, which could be located in the basement of a new building being planned in Whitehall. This was all very well – in fact the plan was approved on 24 March 1938 – but the reality was that such a building would take at least four years to complete.

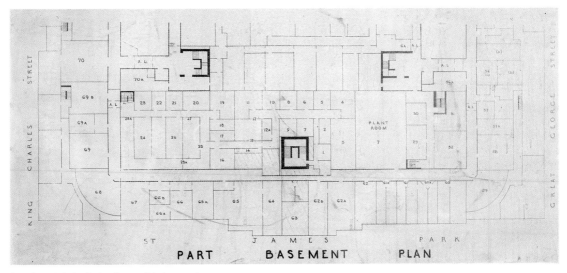

One of the original early plans for use of the basement

Colonel Hastings Ismay wasn't prepared to wait that long. As Deputy Secretary of Britain's Committee of Imperial Defence – a body set up in 1902 to research and advise on matters of military strategy – he was more aware than most of how loudly the clock was ticking. On the morning of 12 March 1938, Hitler had sent his troops into Austria to enforce its incorporation into Nazi Germany. International tensions were soaring, and Ismay could all too easily imagine a German attack on Britain long before any purpose-built war room could be completed.

On 16 March he took matters into his own hands, asking the Office of Works to search for a refuge where the War Cabinet and Chiefs of Staff could carry out their duties in case of emergency. This was the first practical step in the creation of what we now

know as Churchill War Rooms. It was also the first time that anyone had suggested housing Britain's political and military leaders in the same facility. In fact it was only on 4 May 1938 that the Deputy Chiefs of Staff agreed to the idea.

With plans still in this confused and evolving state, news in late May that German troops were massing on the Czechoslovakian border was especially alarming. There might be war any day, but still no war room.

Ismay pressed on with renewed determination. After a rapid survey of available London basements, the Office of Works concluded that the most suitable was underneath the western end of the New Public Offices on Great George Street – conveniently close to Downing Street and Parliament. On 31 May 1938 the site was confirmed. The Chiefs of Staff gave Ismay free rein to create an 'emergency war headquarters' and ordered the Joint Planners to help him.

Right from the start, it was understood that this was just a temporary measure – only to be used if an emergency struck before a permanent war room could be built. 'Nothing very elaborate is contemplated,' Ismay informed the Treasury on 18 June; 'no major structural alterations, no air conditioning or costly gas proofing, and no expensive fittings.'

Ismay's first move was to delegate the day-to-day running of the project to his deputy, Brigadier Leslie Hollis. He in turn called on the help of colleague Lawrence Burgis, with further practical assistance from Eric de Normann of the Office of Works.

'Burgis and I had no precedent to work on,' recalled Hollis. 'This headquarters was to be the first of its type. For a week or two we pored over blueprints of the basement …and considered all the complex arrangements and requirements for which provision had to be made. Eventually we agreed on a plan.'

Over the next couple of months, Hollis, Burgis and de Normann presided over an extraordinary transformation under the streets of Whitehall. Rooms were cleared, alcoves sandbagged, glass doors replaced with teak, brick partitions built, telephone lines installed – and a broadcasting connection was established by the BBC. It was a rapid, improvised process carried out to a brief that shifted constantly as events deteriorated on the Continent.

In September, for example, Hitler sparked a new crisis by threatening to annexe part of Czechoslovakia. Prime Minister Neville Chamberlain, who had taken over from Baldwin in May 1937, attempted to defuse the situation by diplomatic means but matters became so serious that, on 14 September, Ismay ordered that a ventilation system be fitted and made ready in the war rooms. He gave the workmen a week to complete the job. They managed it.

More work followed, including the gas proofing and air conditioning that Ismay had said would not be necessary. On 15 September came a request that the ceilings of the main rooms be strengthened with steel strutting. Two days later the request was extended to all the other rooms too. By 26 September the Central War Room, as the site was now known, was ready for emergency use and Ismay kept a set of keys with him at all times.

On 30 September the crisis on the Continent eased when Hitler signed the Munich Agreement and the Anglo-German Declaration, the latter declaring that Britain and Germany should never go to war with each other again. It was heralded by Chamberlain as a guarantee of 'peace for our time' but dismissed by Churchill as a 'defeat without a war'. Either way, the immediate danger appeared to have passed. The doors of the Central War Room were locked, and the exhausted staff of the Office of Works breathed a sigh of relief.

The Munich Agreement did not bring lasting peace, but it did provide valuable breathing space during which the Central War Room could be expanded and improved. In theory the facility was ready for use;

indeed it had already been manned for a few days during the worst of the so-called Munich Crisis. Hollis had seen enough in that time to have grave concerns about using the rooms for real. The ventilation system was poor, and there was no overnight accommodation, bedding, kitchen, food or washing facilities. Not for nothing did he and others refer to the facility as 'the hole in the ground', or simply 'the hole'.

For the first few months of 1939 Hollis battled unsuccessfully to convince the Office of Works to take action. As late as June the only toilets below ground in the Central War Room were of the 'sand and bucket variety' as one memo put it, and it was only in the last two weeks of August that chemical toilets and two dormitories were added.

The Office of Works carried out these improvements with a great deal of exasperation, frustrated that what had started out as a temporary facility was becoming something closer to semi-permanent. 'We have gone to a great deal of trouble and inconvenience in sacrificing this space,' they reported to Hollis, 'and we look to you to limit your requirements to what are absolutely essential, bearing in mind that the whole scheme is and must be of the nature of a makeshift...'

Makeshift or not, the chances of the Central War Room being used in earnest mounted throughout the summer. With German troops marching into Czechoslovakia in March 1939 tension rose again in Europe, and the officers who had been chosen to man the facility's Map Room were put on alert. A letter sent to Wing Commander John Heagerty, for example, asked him to be available 'at really short notice throughout August and September'

and to 'let us know in advance of any intended absence from your normal address and telephone numbers, since it is impossible to foresee what may occur in Europe'.

Servicemen, politicians, press and public – all knew that it was now a question of when war would come rather than if. Churchill's stock had risen accordingly as his 'alarmist' predictions began to seem more prophetic. Twice, in November 1938, he had been granted the curious honour of being personally attacked by Hitler in speeches. This had prompted a natural reaction in his favour in the British press, and by the summer of 1939 the papers were full of clamour for him to return to the Cabinet.

On Wednesday 23 August Hitler signed a non-aggression pact with the Soviet Union, leaving Germany free to attack Poland – a country which Britain and France had pledged to support. Four days later, officers and staff made their way to the Central War Room, showed their passes to the Royal Marine guards, walked down the stairs to basement level and switched on the lights. It would be six years before these lights were turned off again.

Churchill was summoned out of the political wilderness and into Chamberlain's Cabinet on the afternoon of Friday 1 September, a dozen or so hours after Hitler's troops had invaded Poland. That same day, the Chiefs of Staff took to meeting in the Central War Room. They were in conference there at 11am on Sunday 3 September, when Ismay interrupted their meeting to tell them that the country was at war. They received the news without comment.

The Joint Planners were also at work in the Central War Room that Sunday morning. RAF Officer William Dickson recalls the first hour of the war very well:

> The PM announced that we were at war... [Radar] plots began to appear... enemy raids coming into this country... The sirens went over London... And then an extraordinary thing happened. The white telephone rang – the PM's personal telephone from No. 10... We'd briefed people on what to do when it did ring, but we never thought it would ring this early. It was the PM's secretary... the PM was due to make a speech in the House of Commons... was it safe for him to come out?

> I went into the Chiefs of Staff committee... and gave a brief description... Being splendidly British in every way they thanked me very much and... a couple of minutes later... it was all sorted out. Every single one of these raids was non-existent. It was something to do with switching on the radar.

Later that same day Churchill met with the Prime Minister to discuss what role he would take in the Cabinet. He was pleasantly surprised to be reappointed as First Lord of the Admiralty – a position he had occupied during the First World War. His brief, as political head of the Royal Navy, was to manage the conduct of the war at sea, which turned out to be where most of the action would be during the first few months of the conflict.

Churchill's first speech on returning to the front bench came on 26 September in a debate opened by the Prime Minister himself. According to Conservative MP and diarist Harold Nicolson, Chamberlain's address was uninspiring but Churchill set the chamber alight. 'He sounded every note from deep preoccupation to flippancy, from resolution to sheer boyishness. One could feel the spirits of the House rising with every word... In those twenty minutes Churchill brought himself nearer the post of Prime Minister than he has ever been before.'

Whether or not Churchill was destined for higher office, he certainly had no qualms about venturing beyond his brief at the Admiralty. He fired off memo after memo to Chamberlain on everything from the need to reshuffle the Cabinet to the detailed equipment of the Army in France. He also featured prominently in the minutes from War Cabinet meetings held during this period.

In the absence of air raids, Chamberlain held these meetings above ground at Downing Street or Parliament. Ismay, however, continued to insist on improvements to the Central War Room in case the situation changed. Before the end of September he asked for a bigger room to be made available for Cabinet meetings, forcing the Office of Works to give up a large chamber set aside as their own air raid shelter. By 4 October this room had been prepared and on 21 October it was decided to test it by holding a War Cabinet meeting.

Although it was the first time that Britain's political and military leaders had met in their underground facility, it was far from Churchill's first visit. He had already developed a strong interest in the work of the Map Room, making frequent visits to stay up to speed with events as details poured in from every theatre of the war.

By the time of that first meeting, the Central War Room was operational but overcrowded. Desks were continually being crammed into already occupied rooms, and partitions put up to turn one office into two. It remained unclear exactly what function this underground complex was supposed to perform – exacerbated perhaps by the fact that the War Cabinet hardly made use of the facility at all.

On 29 December 1939 the Cabinet Secretary Edward Bridges was moved to circulate a note stating that 'the Central War Room will in future be known as "the Cabinet War Room"'. Its function would be to maintain and supply 'an up to date general picture of the war in all parts of the world' for the War Cabinet, the Chiefs of Staff and the King, and to provide a 'protected meeting place for the War Cabinet and Chiefs of Staff organisation under air raid conditions'.

Underpinned by this new clarity of purpose, the Cabinet War Room entered 1940 in full working order, but the machinery of government itself was running less smoothly. At least three separate discussions had to be held before decisions could be reached on the most important issues – by the Chiefs of Staff, by the War Cabinet itself, and by a third body called the Committee for Military Co-ordination, set up to act as an intermediary between the two.

As a member of both the War Cabinet and the Military Co-ordination Committee, Churchill chafed at this inefficiency. In January 1940, he complained about the 'awful difficulties which our machinery of war-conduct presents to positive action', and continued: 'I see such immense walls of prevention, all built or building, that I wonder whether any plan will have a chance of climbing over them.'

He wrote as a prolific deviser of plans, schemes and stratagems. Since his restoration to the Admiralty he had advocated attacking Germany's western defences by land and air, dropping mines from aircraft into the Rhine to disrupt the country's main internal supply route, and cutting off German access to Swedish iron ore, which made its way to the country by sea via the Norwegian port of Narvik.

He pursued this last aim with dogged determination, first suggesting that neutral Norwegian waters be mined so that ships carrying iron ore would be forced out into the open sea where they could be sunk, then in late 1939 proposing an expedition to Narvik and an advance into Sweden to occupy the ore fields. But it wasn't until late March 1940 that the War Cabinet agreed to a mix of the two proposals: mining Norwegian waters and occupying Narvik.

Further delays meant that the mining operation didn't begin until 8 April, by which time the Germans were themselves landing in Norway to occupy Narvik. British attempts to dislodge them failed – a humiliating setback with echoes of the botched Gallipoli campaign in the First World War, which had also been advocated by Churchill. This time, however, it was clear to Whitehall insiders that Churchill was not to blame – that the campaign might in fact have proved successful had his advice been followed earlier.

A debate in Parliament on 7 May revealed widespread discontent with Chamberlain's leadership, prompting private discussions over the next two days between the beleaguered Prime Minister and his two potential successors, Churchill and the Foreign Minister Lord Halifax. Chamberlain's preferred candidate was Halifax, but as a peer he would have struggled to lead the government from the House of Lords. When he stepped aside, Churchill remained the only viable option.

Events on 10 May hurried the decision along. Hitler's armies launched a shock offensive in the Low Countries, Chamberlain tendered his resignation, and by 6pm Churchill was Prime Minister. A few days later, as British forces were being driven back towards the French coast, he walked down the stairs to the War Rooms and headed for the Cabinet Room. Brigadier Leslie Hollis recalled the scene many years later:

> As he looked around the empty room, the poignancy of the moment touched him. No one could say what the news would be within the hour, whether or not England was even then under her first invasion in a thousand years. The little group stood for a moment in silence under the humming fans, each thinking his own thoughts, and then Mr Churchill took his cigar out of his mouth and pointed at the homely wooden chair at the head of the table. 'This is the room from which I'll direct the war,' he said slowly.

Churchill had come to his War Rooms.

Winston Churchill seated at his desk in the No 10 Annexe Map Room, May 1945

THE ENTRANCE

The door and stairway that are used to enter Churchill War Rooms today did not exist in wartime. Instead staff entered via the government building above (now the Treasury Building, but then known as the New Public Offices).

To enter the War Rooms, staff would first use this entrance to the New Public Offices on Horse Guards Road opposite St James's Park.

A.R.P
PHONE

Once inside the building, War Rooms personnel would climb another couple of steps before reaching an internal door, shown to the far left of this photo.

Behind this first internal door was Staircase 15, which wound down to the basement level. Having climbed up a number of steps from the street, staff would often take longer than they expected to descend to the basement. This appears to have convinced many that the War Rooms were as much as 50 feet below ground. They were in fact only one floor below ground.

Staircase 15 brought staff into the War Rooms near to where the kitchen is situated in the Churchill Suite. This door was guarded by Royal Marines, which added to a commonly reported impression that going to work in the War Rooms felt like climbing down into the bowels of a ship.

The rather larger door in the centre of this image is the entrance to the No 10 Annexe flat – where Churchill and his family lived from December 1940 onwards – which was immediately above the War Rooms.

Ilene Hutchinson

ENTERING THE WAR ROOMS

Shorthand typist Ilene Hutchinson remembers what it was like to make your way into the War Rooms.

'Security was very tough actually. Entering the building... we had to sign on at the times we were scheduled to sign on, and then just fly down the spiral staircase. We had a Marine just on the left of us as we were going down. He was like a waxwork in Madame Tussaud's, just standing there with his rifle at the ready and his red banded hat and not fluttering an eyebrow. Along a passage after the set of stairs, and down some more stairs and then along to the office... We opened the door quietly because there may have been a flap on... You couldn't burst in like you would in an ordinary office.'

'The higher up the officer, the more likely they were to go along with the checking of passes.'

Frank Higgins, military policeman and former guard at the War Rooms

▶ Gaining access to the War Rooms meant running past a strict set of security checks. Staff were issued with passes like this one (shown front and back), which they were expected to show without fail to the guards as they passed.

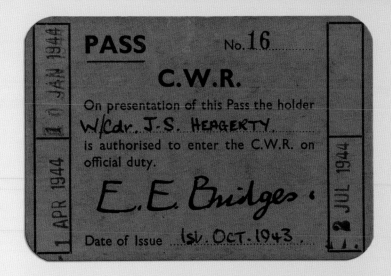

PASS   No. 16

10 JAN 1944

1 APR 1944

2 JUL 1944

C.W.R.

On presentation of this Pass the holder

W/Cdr. J.S. HEAGERTY

is authorised to enter the C.W.R. on official duty.

E. E. Bridges

Date of Issue   1st. OCT. 1943.

This Pass is not transferable. If found, it should be handed in at any Police Station, or sent to—

The Camp Commandant,
2, Storey's Gate Building,
S.W.I.

It must be returned when the holder ceases to have duty in the C.W.R.

Signature of Holder   John J. Heagerty

(S.7518)

THE MAIN CORRIDOR

The main corridor in the War Rooms stretches about 75 metres from one end of the basement to the other, running parallel to Horse Guards Road outside. There were many other corridors to navigate in wartime, but this was the one most frequented by Churchill himself – connecting, as it did, the Cabinet Room, his bedroom, the Map Room, the Transatlantic Telephone Room and many other offices and facilities. Along its walls today there remain many clues to the way that life was conducted underground during the war.

The white metal duct running along the corridor and branching off into every room carried air around the War Rooms. It appears to have served some areas of the basement better than others, with some workers complaining that they suffered from violent headaches because the atmosphere became so foul towards the end of the working day.

The corridors did not merely serve to connect the various sections of the War Rooms together. They also doubled as workplaces when space became especially tight. During the Blitz, for example, typists could be found stationed in some of the alcoves.

The storage chests along the walls of the corridor were used to hold maps that might be required in the Map Room – or more likely by the Joint Planners engaged in devising military strategy for even the most remote theatres of the war.

The main corridor photographed c.1945

'The building to me had masses and masses and masses of corridors. How the heck you ever found your way around I shall never know.'

Leading Aircraftwoman Myra Murden

WAY OUT

To Gᵀ. GEORGE Sᵀ.

THERE IS TO BE NO WHISTLING
OR UNNECESSARY NOISE IN THIS
PASSAGE

▲ This sign gives some indication of the serious work undertaken in the War Rooms, but such rules and regulations were not always observed. One veteran, for example, recalls how Map Room officers celebrated Christmas 1941 by racing toilet rolls along the corridor.

◄ The main entrance to the War Rooms was via Horse Guards Road opposite St James's Park, but the building could also be entered from Great George Street. There were several other emergency exits, some of which involved the use of ceiling hatches and ladders.

GENERAL ISMAY

Apart from Churchill himself, Major-General Sir Hastings Ismay was arguably the most important figure in the story of the War Rooms. Before the war, as Secretary to the Committee of Imperial Defence, it was Ismay who made sure that the underground bunker was ready for action. During the war, as Deputy Secretary (Military) to the War Cabinet and Chief of Staff to Churchill, he was the glue that held the War Rooms together, smoothing over the many tensions that arose between the Prime Minister and his military chiefs. After the war, it was Ismay again who helped ensure that the most important rooms in the basement were preserved for posterity.

In September 1939, Room 61 was partitioned to create Room 61 Right for Ismay and Room 61 Left for his two Private Secretaries. Both rooms were taken over by the Joint Planning Staff in the summer of 1940, but reverted to their original occupants from early 1943 onwards, when they proved especially useful during the V-weapon offensives of 1944 and 1945. The telephone shown here, with its stark cautionary message, is displayed on the desk in Room 61 Left.

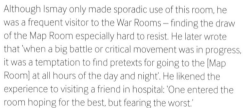
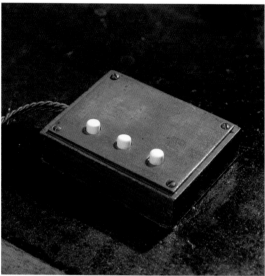

Although Ismay only made sporadic use of this room, he was a frequent visitor to the War Rooms – finding the draw of the Map Room especially hard to resist. He later wrote that 'when a big battle or critical movement was in progress, it was a temptation to find pretexts for going to the [Map Room] at all hours of the day and night'. He likened the experience to visiting a friend in hospital: 'One entered the room hoping for the best, but fearing the worst.'

At the touch of one of these buttons, Ismay could summon his junior officers from their room next door, or connect to the Prime Minister's quarters and the War Cabinet Room.

The addition of carpet to Ismay's room is the most obvious indication that it was used by a senior officer. There are also other differences, such as the desk and the lamp, and the extra-wide bed.

Detail of a document box on display in the room manned by Ismay's Private Secretaries. One of his staff's duties was to establish the administrative arrangements for the Prime Minister's foreign conferences and trips.

▲ A surviving copy of the government's 'C.W.R Standing Instructions' for the War Rooms includes an instruction for heaters like this one to be turned off whenever a room was left empty – an example of wartime economy, even here at the centre of power.

▶ Two officers manned this room to assist Ismay. One was Commander Maurice 'Senior' Knott; the other was Lieutenant Ian McEwan, who was inevitably known as 'Junior'. Wooden props and beams such as those in this room can be seen throughout the War Rooms. They were installed before the war as a crude precaution against the possible collapse of the building above during an air raid.

SIR EDWARD
BRIDGES

As Secretary to the War Cabinet, Sir Edward Bridges was the most senior civil servant in the land. It was his job to call meetings of the War Cabinet, organise the agenda, prepare and circulate minutes and make sure that all of the decisions taken were implemented. Together with Ismay, to whom he delegated all military matters arising from the War Cabinet, Bridges was key to Britain's war effort. The pair were described by Churchill's Private Secretary Sir John Colville as 'the twin pillars on which the Prime Minister rested'.

In autumn 1939, the room allocated to Bridges was partitioned so that it could also accommodate his personal secretary, Sir Ronald Harris, and one or more assistant secretaries.

▲ The right-hand room used by Sir Edward Bridges himself is afforded the luxury of a small carpet, but is otherwise extremely basic. Described by Churchill as 'a man of exceptional force, ability and personal charm', Bridges is said to have adopted an unobtrusive leadership style built on tact, diplomacy and cooperation.

◀ When Bridges' room was partitioned in 1939, the left-hand side was allocated to three of his assistant secretaries, while Bridges shared the right-hand room with his personal secretary Sir Ronald Harris. This arrangement was soon changed so that Harris and one assistant secretary used this left-hand room, leaving Bridges with quarters to himself.

'Sir Edward Bridges, son of a poet, with a poet's unruly hair, a man of shy charm, held his high post with such modesty that he managed to merge his considerable intellect into a balanced whole of unobtrusive leadership and tactful cooperation with colleagues trimmed for war.'

Description of Sir Edward Bridges by Joan Bright Astley, a senior War Rooms secretary

SIR JOHN MARTIN

In 1944 and 1945 Room 66B was occupied by Sir John Martin, Churchill's Principal Private Secretary. It was Martin's role to run the Prime Minister's office, managing his diary, accompanying him to meetings at home and abroad, and dealing with all his incoming and outgoing correspondence. At his desk in this room, he would also act as Churchill's gatekeeper, ensuring that no-one gained undue access to the Prime Minister.

◀ Martin would have made most use of this room during the V-weapon offensive, which saw V1 flying bombs and later V2 rockets target London.

THE
CABINET ROOM

The existence of the entire War Rooms complex was born out of the need to create a safe meeting room where the War Cabinet could convene during enemy bombing raids. Here the Prime Minister, his key ministers and advisers would meet with the Chiefs of Staff to make decisions of extraordinary significance. Here too the Chiefs of Staff would hold their own discussions, and Churchill would chair meetings of the Defence Committee, which he set up on becoming Prime Minister. It is a room which has hardly changed in the decades since, and the details it contains cast a great deal of insight into what it must have been like to attend one of the many fateful meetings held within its spartan confines.

The entrance to the Cabinet Room consists of two doors, both of which were locked and guarded when a meeting was in progress. One sentry stood outside the outer door, the other was posted in the tiny lobby dividing the room from the corridor.

The inner of the two doors leading into the Cabinet Room was fitted with a glass-covered slit. This allowed the sentry to see what was going on inside the room but without being able to hear a word of what was said. Secrecy was paramount.

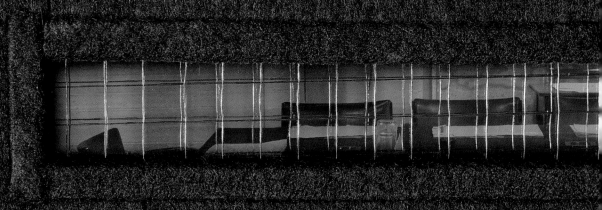

General Sir Hastings Ismay, August 1945

THE WAR CABINET SYSTEM

During the war, General Ismay was asked to write a summary of how the War Cabinet system worked. He had this to say about its meetings:

'The War Cabinet meets every day, sometimes twice a day. The morning meeting invariably starts with reports by the Services on the military situation, and by the Foreign Secretary on political developments. Thereafter the War Cabinet addresses itself to whatever problems may have been put before it, in the shape of strategical reports by the Chiefs of Staff, or memoranda on any and every problem which requires to be resolved, from the Ministers, Committees or Departments concerned.'

The room has been preserved to look the way it would have done moments before a meeting of the War Cabinet held there at 5pm on 15 October 1940. Bombs had caused severe damage to 10 Downing Street the previous evening, and this had finally persuaded Churchill to meet in the War Rooms on a regular basis.

One of the most remarkable features of the room is the way in which the tables have been laid out to create a central well with enough space for three seats. It was in this crucible that the heads of the Army, Navy and Air Force would sit – eyeball to eyeball with the Prime Minister, who would be hunched in the rounded wooden chair opposite. Given Churchill's propensity to push his military chiefs as far beyond their comfort zones as they could bear, it was an arrangement frought with tension and confrontation.

In peacetime any minutes and conclusions arising from a Cabinet meeting were the sole responsibility of the Secretary to the Cabinet. In wartime a succession of Assistant Secretaries would attend different sections of the meetings, and then leave the room to get on with the minuting process. This meant that the minutes and conclusions of a morning meeting of the War Cabinet could be circulated by 3 or 4pm the same day.

The words displayed on the conference table were spoken by Queen Victoria when she was presented with a gloomy report on progress in the Boer War: 'Please understand there is no depression in this house and we are not interested in the possibilities of defeat, they do not exist.' A copy was presented to President George W Bush during his visit to the War Rooms in 2001.

The Cabinet Room photographed c.1945

▲ During meetings in the War Cabinet Room, Churchill is reported to have thrown his cigar butts over his shoulder and into a fire bucket. The story goes that the marine orderlies would collect them up after a meeting and sell them.

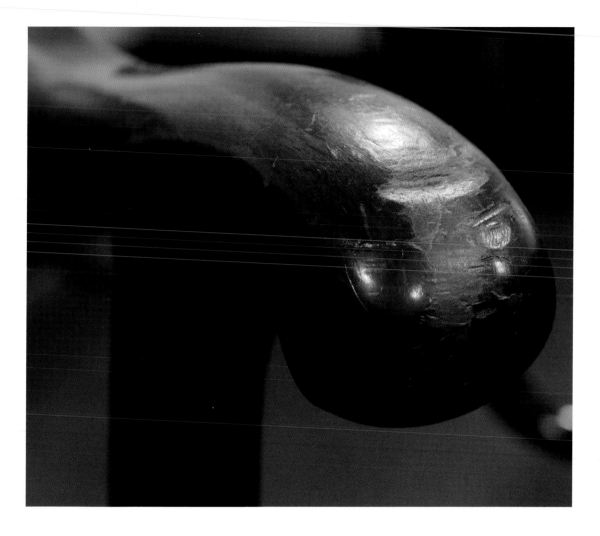

▲ The wooden arms of Churchill's chair are gouged with scratch marks that speak volumes for the nervous energy of its occupant and the tension of the hundreds of meetings that he presided over in this room. The marks differ on each arm. Churchill's right hand appears to have scratched at the wood, while the signet ring on his left made deeper gouges.

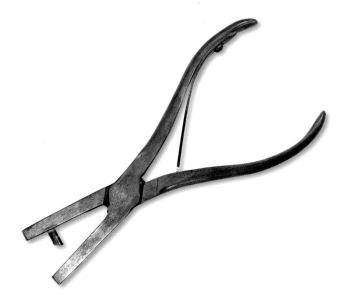

▲ Churchill used to insist that all documents in the War Rooms were punched and tagged rather than stapled or paper-clipped. The device sitting in front of him on the table was his preferred type of hole punch, which he used to refer to as a 'klop'. He didn't always get his way. One member of staff remembers stapling a document and sending it to the Prime Minister, who promptly cut his finger on it.

▶ Like all British government ministers, Churchill used a specially made red box to carry his State papers with him wherever he went. The position of the handle and lock ensured that the box had to be locked before it could be picked up. The Barbados sticker was added by Churchill's son Randolph.

2

THE
DARKEST DAYS

May 1940 to May 1941

hree days after Winston Churchill became Prime Minister, he stood up to address Parliament: 'We have before us many, many long months of struggle and of suffering,' he said. He was right. Hitler's troops were already pushing the British Army back to the Channel, and the French Army was on the verge of disintegration. By 27 May the men of the British Expeditionary Force would be clambering onto boats at Dunkirk and heading back to Britain – a Britain that was about to come under siege.

Continuing his speech Churchill declared: 'You ask, what is our policy? I can say: It is to wage war, by sea, land and air, with all our might and with all the strength that God can give us… You ask, what is our aim? I can answer in one word: It is victory, victory at all costs, victory in spite of all terror, victory, however long and hard the road may be; for without victory, there is no survival.'

They were brave words and well received, but the truth was that the policies and aims of the government were not so set in stone. From 26 to 28 May, as the evacuation from Dunkirk was getting under way, Churchill was locked in tense discussions with his five-man War Cabinet. The agenda was profoundly simple: should Britain fight on or should the government negotiate a peace? Churchill was for fighting, but he faced being out-voted by his colleagues. It was only by gathering support among the more junior members of the government that he carried the day.

By 4 June, the operation at Dunkirk was complete. Against all the odds, over 337,000 British and allied troops had escaped capture – far more than Churchill had dared hope. 'The successful evacuation of the BEF has revolutionised the Home Defence position,' he wrote to Ismay, his spirits lifted by the lifeline, however short-lived, that the evacuation had provided. Anticipating a German invasion he dismissed all talk of a negotiated peace once and for all, telling Parliament: 'We shall fight on the beaches, we shall fight on the landing grounds, we shall fight in the fields and in the streets, we shall fight in the hills; we shall never surrender.'

Churchill projected an infectious sense of confidence, but he was by no means sure of victory. Ten days after this iconic speech, he turned to Ismay and said: 'Do you realise we probably have a maximum of three months to live?' It was a remark made in good humour but it gives some indication of the private burden that he was carrying. He also became so uncharacteristically brusque with staff at the War Rooms and 10 Downing Street that, on 23 June, his wife Clementine was moved to write him a letter, warning him 'that there is a danger of your being generally disliked by your colleagues and subordinates because of your rough sarcastic and overbearing manner'. Fearing how her words would be received, she promptly tore the letter up but then decided to send it to him after all.

Churchill wasn't the only one feeling the pressure. Following the fall of France, staff at the War Rooms were struggling to adjust to new priorities. In the months since the start of the war, the layout and function of the underground facility had become relatively well established – although not without a good deal of change and experimentation. Two chief purposes had emerged: to gather intelligence on the war, and to provide an emergency meeting place for the War Cabinet and the Chiefs of Staff.

The heart of the underground complex throughout the war – and at any hour of day or night – was the Map Room. It was here that information on every development in every theatre of the war was gathered, collated and presented on the maps adorning its walls. It was from here too that a daily summary of the war was distributed every morning to the Prime Minister, the Chiefs of Staff and the King, and an intelligence briefing given to the Chiefs of Staff before they went into conference.

Given the importance of the Map Room, the Chiefs of Staff found it convenient to carry out most of their conferences in the underground rooms. This in turn made it useful for their administrative staff to work on site, and for the Joint Planners to stay in close attendance. By the time Churchill became Prime Minister a suite of 15 rooms was in use, providing working and living accommodation for some 60 people. It was a bigger facility than had originally been planned, but it would prove to be nowhere near big enough.

After the fall of France, the risk of a German invasion made it imperative to establish an Advanced Headquarters for Britain's Home Forces at the War Rooms. That way, the Prime Minister and Chiefs of Staff could have direct access to the Commander-in-Chief of the Home Forces. A hasty reorganisation saw this Advanced Headquarters housed in Rooms 62, 62A and 62B. The Map Room Annexe was handed over to Home Forces intelligence officers and a quarter of the Map Room – the holiest of holies – was also set aside for their use.

Alan Brooke, the newly appointed Commander-in-Chief of the Home Forces, visited his underground office on 29 July. After the war he described the set-up

Winston Churchill visits bombed-out buildings in the East End of London on 8 September 1940

as excellent but, mindful of Churchill's capacity for interference, he identified one fault: 'its proximity to Winston!' This was demonstrated from day one, with Brooke's diary recording that he was invited by the Prime Minister to attend part of the War Cabinet meeting – the first to be held in the War Rooms since Churchill had taken office. Brooke described the experience as 'interesting', but the two men would go on to have many clashes around the same table.

By the time of Brooke's appointment Churchill had made several changes to the way in which the war was run. He had pared his War Cabinet down to five men, with the service ministers and Chiefs of Staff attending as required. This was now the forum for discussing any problem, military or civil, on which a decision could only be reached at the highest level. There were other changes too. Churchill combined the office of Prime Minister with the Minister of Defence and established various committees through which he could enjoy direct contact with his Chiefs of Staff. As a result he could now exercise direct supervision not only over military policy and planning, but also the day-to-day conduct of operations.

Yet powerful as he was, Churchill was no dictator. Sir Ian Jacob, the Military Assistant Secretary to the War Cabinet, recalled how the Prime Minister 'pushed and pushed and pushed, which was all to the good provided he had people to keep him on the rails'. If he disagreed with the advice of his Chiefs of Staff, he would argue his case strenuously, but if they held their ground, he would almost always give them his backing. It was this combination of push and pull, according to Jacob, that helped to win the war.

Shortly after becoming Prime Minister, Churchill was given his own bedroom study in the War Rooms, right next door to the Map Room. The expectation that he might soon have need of such a refuge was easily understandable. Throughout August 1940, RAF fighter squadrons were engaging Luftwaffe bombers and fighters in the skies over southern England. Dubbed the Battle of Britain, it was seen as the prelude to the German invasion, which was expected at almost any moment. Until 7 September the chief targets attacked by the Germans were the RAF's forward air bases and coastal defences, but they then switched attention to bombing London itself.

This was the Blitz – the sustained aerial bombardment that Britain's political and military leaders had long expected. It was fear of such a bombardment that had led to the preparation of the War Rooms, and the full capabilities of the facility would be put to the most severe of tests over the course of the next nine months. In September it played host to most evening meetings of the War Cabinet, and in October and November almost every top-level meeting was held there – whether of the War Cabinet, the Defence Committee or the Chiefs of Staff.

On 11 September, just days after the beginning of the Blitz, the Prime Minister made use of the War Rooms' broadcasting facilities for the first time. Sitting at his bedroom desk, he gave one of his most stirring orations – condemning the bombing raids on London and the south-east, giving a stark warning about the possibility of invasion, and issuing a rallying cry for every man and woman to do their duty.

The bombing raids were becoming uncomfortably close. The Ministry of Transport, just a short walk away from the War Rooms, was damaged on 12 September, and Buckingham Palace, just on the other side of St James's Park, was dive-bombed the following evening. In fact, news of this attack was handed to the Prime Minister in the War Rooms, while he was presiding over an evening meeting of the War Cabinet.

On 16 September, as the raids continued, Churchill was persuaded to stay the night in his subterranean bedroom for the first time. He did not enjoy the experience. In fact he loathed the idea of seeking out shelter during an attack, preferring if possible to stay above ground or, better still, to find a rooftop from which to view proceedings. By the end of the war, he is thought to have spent only a handful of nights in his War Rooms bed.

During the first few days of the Blitz, however, Churchill and his staff found themselves underground rather more than they would have liked. Churchill's private secretary, John Colville, noted in his diary that 'much of the time, both by day and by night, is being spent in the disagreeable atmosphere of the Central War Room'. Churchill too seemed resigned to the prospect, writing to Neville Chamberlain on 21 September that he proposed 'to lead a troglodyte existence'.

In truth, Churchill lived the life of a nomad, working and staying the night in a variety of locations – 10 Downing Street, Parliament, his country home of Chequers and the War Rooms. On several evenings he also made use of the London Underground offices situated at the disused Down Street station, complete with hot running water, fully plumbed toilet system and well-stocked wine cellar.

For the rest of the War Rooms staff, a night spent underground was somewhat less comfortable. Beneath the War Rooms lies another floor that stretches the full length and breadth of the building above. Its ceiling was uncomfortably low and you had to stoop to get through its doorways, many of which were no more than four feet high. It was known unaffectionately as 'the dock'.

Every night dozens of staff, wrapped modestly in their all-enveloping dressing gowns, would duck their way down the steps, carrying their sheets to any free bed they could find in the spartan dormitories below. Despite the exhaustion brought on by their long working hours, sleep did not always come easily. Some were disturbed by the rattle and hum of the air conditioning system, which seemed to have little effect on the heat or the fug of cigarette smoke. Others were kept awake by the scamperings of rats and bugs, or by the foul smell of the chemical toilets positioned behind crudely constructed screens. It is little wonder that many sought out quiet spots to sleep in the floors above – despite the danger and noise of the Luftwaffe's bombs. Others even preferred to risk the journey home instead.

The increased reliance on the War Rooms as a refuge made it all the more alarming when Churchill discovered late in September 1940 that the site itself was not, as he had assumed, bomb-proof. He immediately ordered the construction of a thick concrete slab above the ceiling, and the addition of an exterior apron wall at ground-floor level. He also insisted that a valuable section of the underground space near the Map Room Annexe be filled in with cement because it was located beneath a staircase and was therefore more vulnerable to attack. Churchill's interest in this slab did not end with the issue of the order for its construction. His was a much more hands-on role, as his private secretary John Colville recalls:

> I remember two or three times having to go with him in the evenings with torches down to where they were putting up traverses and other brickwork in the basement in order to make the building stronger. And he used to go along and comment on them. There was one great occasion when he climbed up on one of the traverses...jumped down the other side...and landed in a pool of liquid cement, which I thought rather funny! I looked over the wall at him and I said: 'I think, sir, that you have met your Waterloo.'

However inconvenient and noisy it was to have workmen crawling all over the site, everyone could see the necessity for the work. In fact, matters became more urgent following a raid on 14 October when shockwaves from nearby blasts caused damage to the Prime Minister's residence at 10 Downing Street. It was this incident that persuaded Churchill to hold meetings in the War Rooms on a more regular basis, beginning with the War Cabinet meeting at 5pm on 15 October. This is the moment in time captured on all the clocks in Churchill War Rooms today.

The same incident also prompted confirmation of a plan to move the Prime Minister's offices and living quarters to the building above the War Rooms (now the Treasury Building). These quarters, which would become known as the No 10 Annexe, were relatively strongly built and gave Churchill direct access to the War Rooms beneath. The move also helped the Prime Minister's staff pin him down in one main location rather than try to predict where he might choose to work, eat and sleep from one day to the next. His movements had become so difficult to track that several of his staff were taken in by a mock minute prepared by his private secretary John Peck at the end of October:

> Action This Day
>
> Pray let six new offices be fitted for my use, in Selfridge's, Lambeth Palace, Stanmore, Tooting Bec, the Palladium and Mile End Road. I will inform you at 6 each evening at which office I shall dine work and sleep. Accommodation will be required for Mrs Churchill, two shorthand-typists, three secretaries and Nelson [the No.10 cat]. There should be a shelter for all and a place for me to watch air-raids from the roof. This should be completed by Monday. There is to be no hammering during office hours, that is between 7am and 3am.
>
> WSC

The Churchills moved into the No 10 Annexe in December 1940. The onset of winter – and the losses sustained by the Luftwaffe during the Battle of Britain – meant that the prospect of an invasion now seemed much less likely. Nonetheless, the chances of a British victory remained remote, and the spring of 1941 brought no relief. Bombs continued to rain down over London night after night, while workmen below the

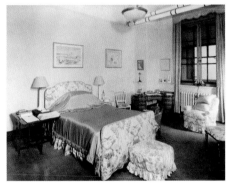

Annexe extended the concrete slab to bring steadily more rooms under its protection. By the beginning of May 1941, a further 34 rooms had been made available. This meant that a telephone exchange, first-aid room and canteen could be added, as well as a suite of rooms for the emergency use of the Prime Minister and his wife, personal staff and key ministers.

As it turned out, London suffered the last heavy raid of the Blitz on 10 May, so the rooms in the 'Churchill Suite' were rarely used. After nine long months of bombing, Hitler was ready to launch an invasion – but it would not be an assault on Britain. Instead he was about to turn his attention to the Soviet Union, in what would prove to be one of the most pivotal decisions in the war.

Top From December 1940 onwards the Prime Minister and his wife lived mainly in the No 10 Annexe flat, adapted from ground floor offices directly above the Cabinet War Rooms. Mrs Churchill decorated the flat in attractive colours and with their own pictures and furniture, but when possible they entertained in 10 Downing Street.
Bottom Clementine Churchill's bedroom in the No 10 Annexe.

THE DOCK

Despite its low ceilings and poor ventilation, the sub-basement below the War Rooms — known as the 'dock' — was also put to use during the war, when pressure for room in the main basement level became more acute.

Museum records reveal that all sorts of items were found in the sub-basement when IWM began work on restoring the floor above. There were sinks, fire buckets, stepladders, stretchers, ink bottles, mail bags, in-trays and much more — reflecting the wider use to which the dock was put during the war. Many of the objects were used in the restoration of the War Rooms, but many others are now held in storage.

Most of the doorways in the dock were extremely low, forcing staff to stoop to get through. The addition of ventilation trunking in the sub-basement further reduced the ceiling height in many of the rooms, and added a constant low-level noise to the list of irritants for staff.

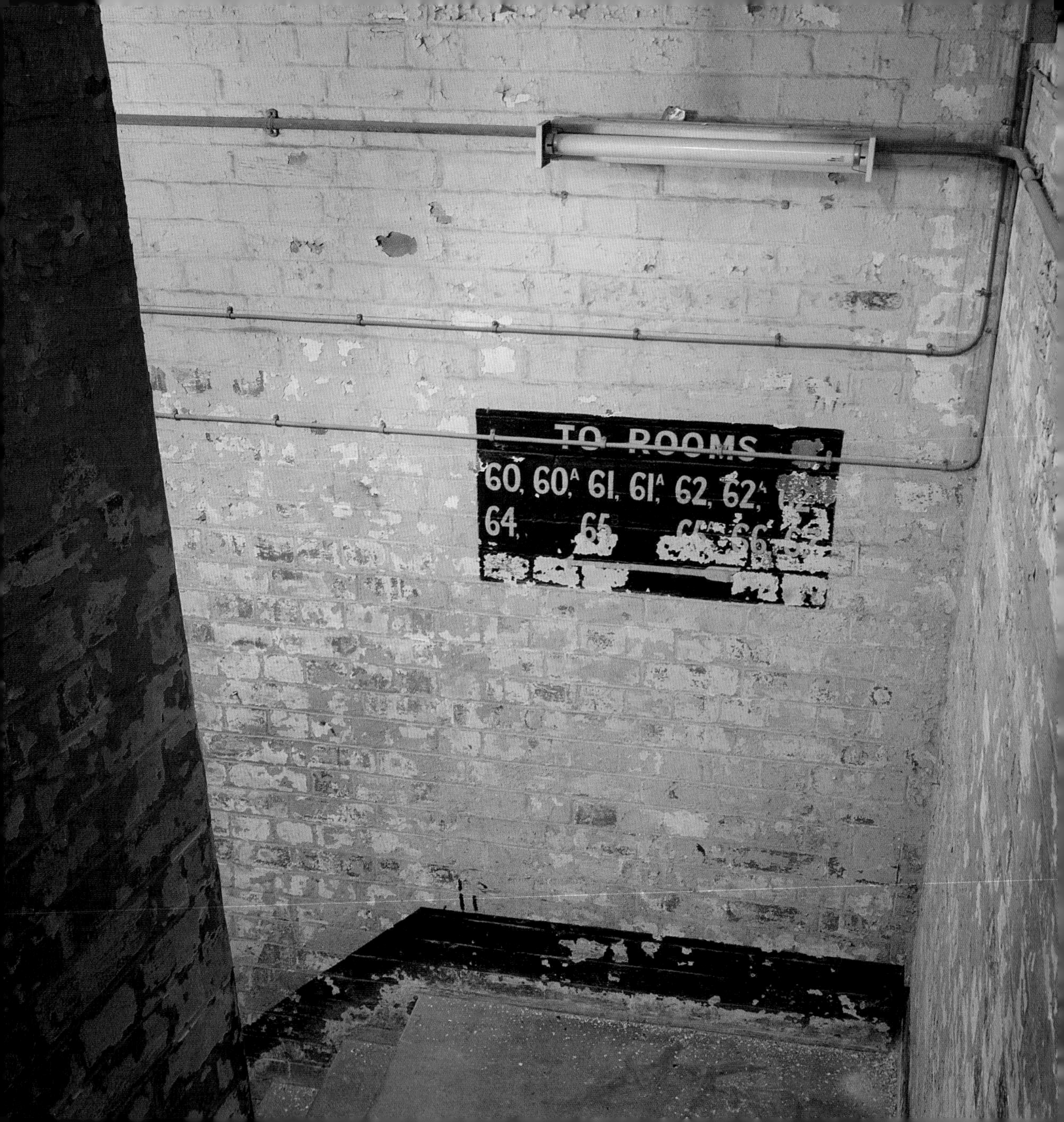
TO ROOMS
60, 60A 61, 61A 62, 62A
64, 65 66

Elizabeth Layton

▲ According to the Standing Instructions for March 1943 there were 22 of these chemical toilets in the sub-basement – 13 set aside for men, 9 for women. Anyone who wanted to use plumbed-in toilets had to head up two floors, watched all the way by the ever-present Royal Marine guards.

◄ For the most part the dock was reserved for overnight accommodation, which meant it saw intensive use during the Blitz of 1940–1941 and the V-weapon offensive of 1944–1945. But some unfortunate staff had to make the trip down the stairs every day – not to grab some sleep, but to work in the most dismal of offices.

SLEEPING IN THE DOCK

One of Churchill's secretaries, Elizabeth Layton, describes what it was like to sleep down in the dock:

'When sleeping in the shelter after late duty, one would retire to the bathroom in the floor above to put on one's night attire (taken from the suitcase out of which one lived) and hurry down several flights of stairs, past the War Rooms to the bedroom level below. By this time one was safely past meeting anyone. But when, having slept heavily for six hours, to the roar of the air-conditioning, in a narrow cot covered with army blankets, one would emerge from one's room, there were all sorts of people whom one wished to avoid. As one hurried up the stairs, heavy-eyed, in one's dressing gown, one always seemed to meet the sprucest, haughtiest, most glamorous officers coming the other way.'

Sleeping quarters and emergency kitchen photographed c.1945

Although the War Rooms staff were grateful to have accommodation provided, few of them found it easy to sleep in the uncomfortable surroundings of the dock. The air conditioning rattled and hummed, and did little to improve the smoky, hot and humid atmosphere. The smell of chemical toilets wafted up and down the corridors, while rats and bugs were often seen scuttling across floors and beds.

THE
BROADCASTING
ROOM

The decision to install broadcasting equipment was taken very early on in the planning of the War Rooms. After the war the room was stripped, but its contents have since been carefully restored. Mr H J Gregory, one of the BBC engineers who worked here during the war, acted as an adviser on the project.

The machinery in Room 60 Left made it possible for Churchill to make four major speeches from his bedroom study. The first was on 11 September 1940, exhorting Britons to prepare for a German invasion. The second was a broadcast to the French Empire on 21 October 1940, and the third to the people of Italy two months later. The last came on 8 December 1941 in response to the Japanese attack on the US fleet at Pearl Harbor.

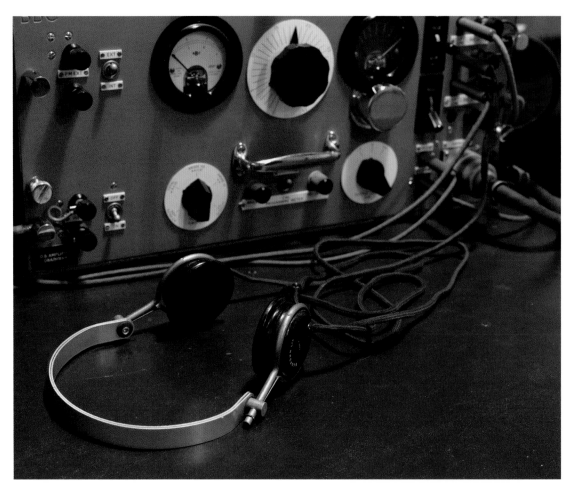

▲ BBC technicians arranged for microphones to be set up in the Prime Minister's bedroom study and in the Cabinet Room. The latter involved suspending the microphone from an ingenious counter-balanced contraption above the Prime Minister's chair – a sketch of which can be found in the museum's files. According to Mr H J Gregory, who assisted with broadcasts from the Cabinet War Rooms during the war, Churchill would usually call for a broadcast at very short notice. The team would only find out at the last minute whether it was to be made from the War Rooms, 10 Downing Street or Chequers. Luckily it took no time at all to prepare the equipment.

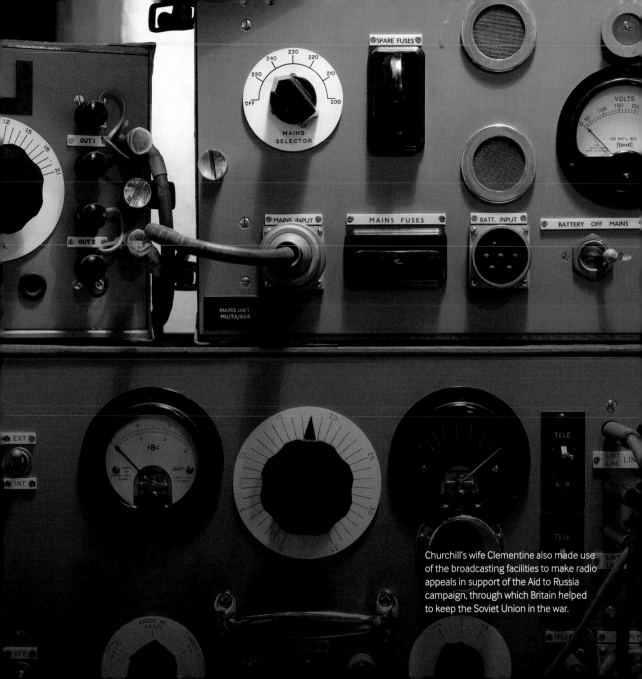

Churchill's wife Clementine also made use of the broadcasting facilities to make radio appeals in support of the Aid to Russia campaign, through which Britain helped to keep the Soviet Union in the war.

No one should blind himself to the fact that a heavy full-scale invasion of this island is being prepared with all the usual German thoroughness and method and that it may be launched at any time now upon England, upon Scotland, or upon Ireland, or upon all three. If this invasion is going to be tried at all, it does not seem that it can be long delayed... Therefore, we must regard the next week or so as a very important week for us in our history. It ranks with the days when the Spanish Armada was approaching the Channel and Drake was finishing his game of bowls, or when Nelson stood between us and Napoleon's Grand Army at Boulogne. We have read about all this in the history books, but what is happening now is on a far greater scale and of far more consequence to the life and future of the world and its civilisation than those brave old days of the past. Every man and woman will therefore prepare himself and herself to do his duty whatever it may be, with special pride and care.'

Extract from a speech broadcast by Churchill from the War Rooms on 11 September 1940

GHQ,
HOME FORCES

In spring 1940 a General Headquarters for Britain's Home Forces was set up at St Paul's School in Hammersmith, a couple of miles away from the War Rooms. Its staff would be responsible for coordinating the defence of Britain in the unlikely event – or so it seemed at the time – of a German invasion. After the fall of France, the threat of invasion became all too real, and arrangements were made to establish an Advanced Headquarters for the Home Forces in the War Rooms. That way the Prime Minister and Chiefs of Staff would be able to communicate directly with the Commander-in-Chief of the Home Forces. Hasty preparations were therefore made to free up Rooms 62, 62A and 62B for this purpose.

Six senior Home Forces officers worked in Room 62A, displacing several members of the Joint Planning Staff who had used the room for a few months at the beginning of 1940. This room later became a Mess Room for the Royal Marines. Room 62 was fitted out as an office for junior members of the Home Forces staff. Four other rooms were also made available in the sub-basement – a signals room for seven members of staff, a cipher room, and two offices housing 15 clerks between them. Little is known about how these rooms were actually laid out during their occupation by the Home Forces, but CWR historians do know that five junior officers were expected to work in this space.

On His Majesty's Service

◀ To cope with any attempted invasion, the officers stationed in this Advanced Headquarters needed to be in constant contact with the General Headquarters for the Home Forces in Hammersmith – and with all their individual Home Forces units. To help make this possible, a tent was erected in St James's Park to accommodate ten signal despatch riders.

▼ Stirrup pumps like this one were designed to help deal with any outbreaks of fire. It took two or three people to operate – one to direct the nozzle, a second to pump the water from a bucket (kept full at all times), and ideally a third to replenish the bucket.

General Sir Alan Brooke, c.1941

GENERAL SIR ALAN BROOKE

As Commander-in-Chief of Britain's Home Forces, General Sir Alan Brooke was responsible for defending the country against German invasion. In this diary entry from 15 September 1940 he describes the burden he carried:

'Still no move on the part of the Germans! Everything remains keyed up for an early invasion... The coming week must remain a critical one... The suspense of waiting is very trying, especially when one is familiar with the weakness of our defence!... A responsibility such as that of the defence of this country under the existing conditions is one that weighs on one like a ton of bricks, and it is hard at times to retain the hopeful, confident exterior which is so essential to retain the confidence of those under one, and to guard against their having any doubts as regards final success.'

Between July 1940 and January 1941 Room 62B acted as the emergency accommodation for General Sir Alan Brooke, at that time the Commander-in-Chief of the Home Forces. It was later assigned to the 'Camp Commandant', the man responsible for the day-to-day maintenance of the War Rooms. This key rack, containing keys to every room in the complex, dates back to that part of the room's occupation.

THE MAP ROOM
ANNEXE

Room 64 is one of the few areas in the War Rooms that fulfilled much the same purpose throughout the war. Situated next door to the main Map Room, it was referred to as its Annexe. It became a focal point for the growing number of Joint Planning Staff officers who could not be accommodated in the Map Room, but who nonetheless needed access to its maps.

Today the Map Room Annexe acts more like a corridor than a room, but it is actually arranged in much the same way as it appeared during the war. It also contains several features that give an insight into its original use.

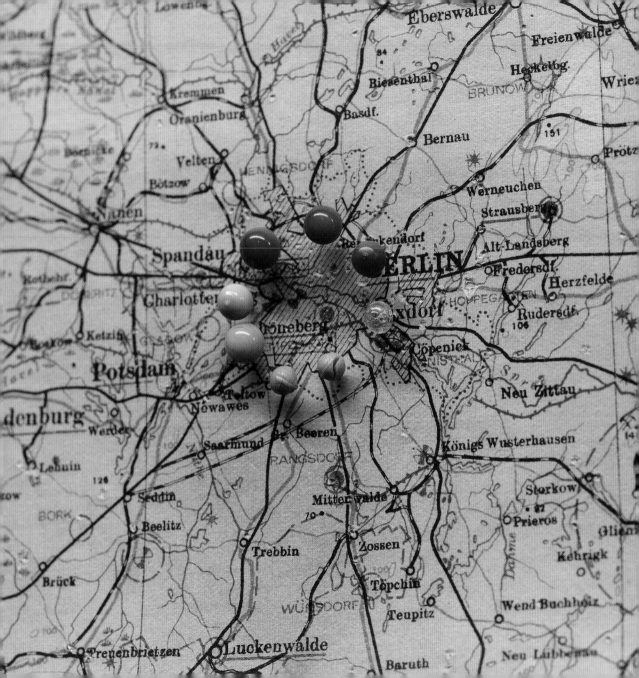

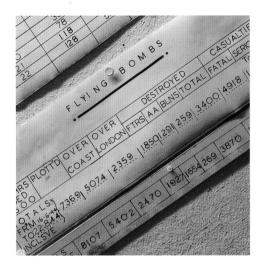

▲ Part of the work of the Joint Planning and Joint Intelligence Staff was to collate, analyse and issue reports on all sorts of aspects of the war. This table was compiled to record the effects of the first two months of V1 'flying bomb' attacks in 1944.

▶ This telephone switch frame allowed officers in the War Rooms to make secure phone calls from their rooms. Only one scrambling device was available for such calls, so this switch frame was installed to allow the officers to share its use.

The large map on one wall of the Annexe spent
much of the war hanging in the main Map Room.
It charts in great detail the devastating advance
of the German forces in Russia in 1941–1942 and
their gradual retreat in the years that followed.

◀ The map also shows the boundaries imposed on Eastern Europe in 1945 – a clue to one of the later preoccupations of the Joint Planning Staff as they looked ahead to the uncertainties of the post-war world.

▼ The main air conditioning system installed in the War Rooms was never especially efficient, so in some places it was supplemented by the addition of American Frigidaire units. There was one each in the Map Room and the Map Room Annexe, and several more were installed elsewhere in the basement.

INTERNAL
DEFENCES

The War Rooms faced two main threats during the war – the possibility of a bomb strike, and an attack on Whitehall by airborne German troops. At intervals around the site you can see clues to the type of defence precautions that were put in place to protect the command centre.

If the War Rooms came under ground attack, the bulk of its defence would be carried out by a platoon of Grenadier Guards permanently stationed at its main entrance, one floor up in the building above. The entrances at basement level would be manned by the Royal Marine orderlies who undertook a variety of day-to-day duties around the site. Any Map Room or Joint Planning officers were expected to arm themselves from gun racks like this one, muster outside the Map Room or Room 62B and then act as a reserve for the Marines. The Camp Commandant or the Map Room Duty Officer would direct the defence, using the Map Room as a command headquarters.

▲ When Churchill discovered in autumn 1940 that the War Rooms were not bomb-proof, he ordered the construction of a concrete slab between the basement ceiling and the ground floor of the building above. A cross-section of part of this slab can be seen in the War Rooms today, complete with its steel waffle containment and support girders.

▶ This section of the War Rooms was filled in with concrete in the winter of 1940 as part of efforts to make the complex more bomb-resistant. When a bomb fell close by later in the war, sending shockwaves through the building, Churchill remarked: 'A pity it was not a bit nearer, so that we might have tested our defences.'

SCHEDULE of ALARM SIG

MEANING	SIGNA
FIRE IN C.W.R.	AUDIBLE BLAST

AIR RAID WARNINGS
    ALERT *(RED)*
    ALL CLEAR *(GREEN)*
IMMINENT DANGER OVERHEAD
IMMINENT DANGER OVERHEAD, PASSED.
	NONE (SIREN c
	NONE (SIREN c
	ELECTRIC BELL *I*
	ELECTRIC BELL c

(GAS) ALARM CLEAR	RATTLES HAND BELLS
GROUND ATTACK FROM OUTSIDE OR INSIDE THE BUILDING. ATTACK BEING MADE	 KLAXON-*CONTINUO* *TWO MINUTES DUR*
ALL CLEAR	MESSAGE BY T

Every member of staff at the War Rooms was expected to make themselves familiar with the Standing Instructions – a set of instructions explaining what to do in case of various emergencies. This 'schedule of alarm signals' was also posted up on one of the walls as a reminder, detailing the meaning of all the whistles, bells, rattles and klaxons that might suddenly begin to sound out.

The alarm signal for a ground attack was a two-minute long blast on a klaxon horn. If it sounded, any women trained to provide First Aid were expected to head to the First Aid room that was added to the site in spring 1941. All telephonists were told to report to the Switchboard room, while all other women were advised to remain at their posts or stay in their rooms. Any unarmed men were told to gather next door to the Cabinet Room and await further instructions.

All War Rooms staff were also instructed to keep their gas masks to hand at all times and to listen out for the sounding of a rattle in the corridors – the agreed warnings for such attacks.

They were also told to keep a complete change of clothes in the War Rooms, to put on in case the clothing they were wearing became contaminated.

MOCK ATTACK

Sir John Winnifrith was Assistant Secretary and Establishment Officer at the War Rooms from 1942 to 1944. Here he describes how he was asked to join the Home Guard in a mock attack on the War Rooms, which exposed weaknesses in the site's defences:

'Well, it was terribly satisfactory from the point of view of the Home Guard. We'd brought ladders with us and it so happened that the defending platoon had chosen to deploy themselves in Great George Street. This left the coast entirely clear [on the other side] and we rushed forward, got our ladders up and in no time got in through the windows. Admittedly the fact that the windows were unguarded and that there was no-one there in the rooms at the time was an accident, and if a German parachute attack or an invasion had been in the offing undoubtedly more would have been done to provide defences at this point. It was terribly satisfying for us as attackers to be marching round the corridors of the war cabinet office ready to slaughter anything in sight... I think any report of our activities would be most unlikely to have reached the ears of the Prime Minister!'

▶ Fortunately the War Rooms staff never had to act on the advice given on this sign. The closest the site came to a direct hit was in September 1940, when a bomb left a crater near the Clive Steps where the entrance to the War Rooms now stands.

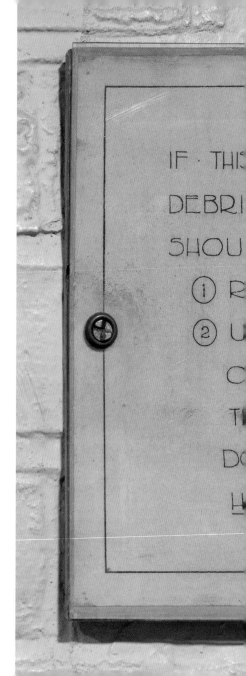

DOOR · SHOULD · BE · BLOCKED · BY
ON · THE · OUTSIDE · THE · OCCUPANTS
:~
EASE · THE · LOCKING · HANDLES
· THESE · CROWBARS · TO · LEVER
N · THE · DOOR · BY · INSERTING
· FLATTENED · ENDS · BETWEEN
R · AND · FRAME · AT · THE · RIGHT
D SIDE · AND · THE · THRESHOLD

CHURCHILL'S ROOM

On 27 July 1940 this room was set aside for Winston Churchill. He is known to have slept overnight here only a couple of times during the war, but he used the room as an office before and after meetings with the War Cabinet or Chiefs of Staff, and he is thought to have enjoyed some of his famous afternoon naps here too. It was also the backdrop to four of his wartime radio broadcasts, using the BBC microphones arranged on his desk. The room was preserved after the war, but some of the furniture has since been rearranged to accommodate the addition of the glass wall on one side.

Churchill's bedroom was large by the standards of the War Rooms (it was originally intended to be the meeting room for the War Cabinet before another even larger room was freed up). It was also supremely well positioned next door to the Map Room, where Churchill would often drop in to catch up on the latest developments.

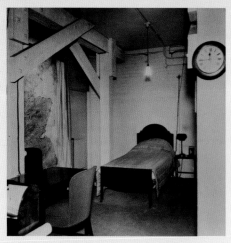

Churchill's Room photographed c.1945

THE DICTATOR

Churchill was well known for his unusual working practices. Here the Prime Minister's Private Secretary Sir John Colville recalls a scene that took place in his War Rooms bedroom in November 1940:

'I remember vividly going into his bedroom down there one evening and it was just when Neville Chamberlain died and he was dictating to Mrs Hill, one of his personal secretaries, a very moving speech, which he made the next day in the House of Commons.

And [he did] that certainly... lying flat on his bed looking, I think, not totally proper because he did rather forget who was in the room... He dictated quite a lot from that room — quite a lot of his speeches — because he liked to lie in bed and dictate.'

▶ When Churchill became Prime Minister, he told George Rance never to let the clocks tell the wrong time. According to Leslie Hollis, Rance only failed in his job once, when the clock in the Cabinet Room stopped one evening in June 1943. Churchill was quick to take Rance to task.

Perhaps surprisingly, the bed provided for
Churchill was of the standard small Civil Service
type seen all over Whitehall. He is nonetheless
known to have spent the night here three times.

'Whatever else history may or may not say about these terrible, tremendous years, we can be sure that Neville Chamberlain acted with perfect sincerity according to his lights and strove to the utmost of his capacity and authority, which were powerful, to save the world from the awful, devastating struggle in which we are now engaged. This alone will stand him in good stead as far as what is called the verdict of history is concerned.'

Extract from a speech by Churchill marking the death of his predecessor Neville Chamberlain — said to have been composed while lying on his bed in the War Rooms.

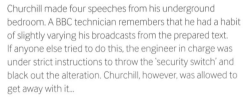

Churchill made four speeches from his underground bedroom. A BBC technician remembers that he had a habit of slightly varying his broadcasts from the prepared text. If anyone else tried to do this, the engineer in charge was under strict instructions to throw the 'security switch' and black out the alteration. Churchill, however, was allowed to get away with it...

The desk assigned to Churchill was unusually wide. On its leather-topped surface sat a device with three buttons on it so that the Prime Minister could call on the services of his detective, butler or private secretary as required.

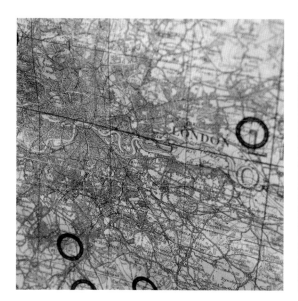

A series of maps on the walls showed Britain's main coastal and air defence installations, as well as possible landing sites for a German invasion – the Prime Minister's chief concern in the dark days of 1940. Curtains were provided so that the maps could be discreetly covered while Churchill was entertaining visitors.

Sitting within easy reach of the Prime Minister's bed was an emergency lamp in case of any electrical problem. There were also a couple of candles available on the desk, although no such loss of power ever took place.

3

THE
TIDE TURNS

June 1941 to December 1943

On 22 June 1941, the colourful bank of telephones in the Map Room – known as the 'beauty chorus' – brought dramatic news to the Cabinet War Rooms. The German Army had invaded the Soviet Union. The reports came as no surprise to the occupants of Churchill's underground bunker. Over the course of the previous few months, they had received repeated intelligence of Hitler's plans. Churchill had tried to warn Stalin as early as 3 April, and despite his long-held antipathy to Communism he was poised to welcome the Soviet Union as a new, if unlikely, ally. Talking to his private secretary John Colville the night before the invasion, he remarked that 'if Hitler invaded Hell, I would make at least a favourable reference to the devil in the House of Commons'. And in a radio address the following night, he made it clear that 'any man or state who fights against Nazidom will have our aid'.

In common with most informed observers, Churchill did not expect his new ally to fare any better against

the rampant German Army than had the French, Polish, Yugoslavs, Greeks and, indeed, the British. The only fighting partner that Churchill longed to have in his corner was the United States, and he spent much of 1941 courting their support. After some negotiation, in March a 'Lend Lease' agreement was passed, through which the US would go on to supply as much as a quarter of all Britain's munitions. And in August, he hoped to make further progress by meeting with Roosevelt in person. It was an arrangement steeped in secrecy. Roosevelt set off for a 'fishing trip' in Maine and then boarded a US cruiser to journey to Placentia Bay in Newfoundland. Churchill meanwhile travelled by his specially converted armoured train as far as Thurso in Scotland and then boarded the battleship HMS *Prince of Wales* to make a speedy Atlantic crossing.

Back in London, the staff of the War Rooms were forced to adjust to life without the Prime Minister, two of the three Chiefs of Staff and several other key advisers and aides. There could be no pause in activity; reports still had to be prepared, plans made and decisions taken. Deputies took on extra responsibilities, tasks were delegated and long-distance lines of communication were established and put to the test. It was a sign of things to come, for what seemed atypical during those two weeks in August 1941 would become commonplace in the years ahead.

Churchill returned to Britain with little of substance to show for the meeting. He was glad to have had the chance to make a personal impression on Roosevelt, but it was clear that words alone would not be enough to bring the US into the war. Over the course of the next hundred days or so Churchill projected his usual confidence in victory – he made use of his famously ebullient 'V' sign for the first time at around this period – but the truth was that he was waiting for something to happen. On 7 December, something did.

The surprise Japanese attack on the US fleet at Pearl Harbor triggered a sudden escalation of the war. Broadcasting from the War Rooms the following evening, Churchill condemned the 'base and brutal' actions of the Japanese and warned of further dangers to come. But, leaning into the microphone on the desk of his bedroom study, he signed off his address by looking forward to a brighter future:

> In the past we had a light which flickered, in the present we have a light which flames, and in the future there will be a light which will shine calm and resplendent over all the land and all the sea!

Despite Churchill's confidence, this new phase of the war brought disaster upon disaster for Britain and its Empire. While the US fleet burned at Pearl Harbor, the Japanese were attacking British territories across the Far East by land, sea and air. On 10 December, HMS *Prince of Wales* – the battleship that had carried Churchill to Newfoundland in August – was hit by Japanese torpedoes and sunk off the coast of Malaya. It was grim news to receive as Churchill boarded her sister ship HMS *Duke of York* to journey to Washington two days later.

It was a difficult time too for the Prime Minister himself. Unknown to all but his closest aides, he suffered a heart attack during the trip to Washington and by the time he returned to Britain, he faced a vote of confidence in the House of Commons. It is not hard to understand the concerns of his fellow MPs. Almost two years into Churchill's premiership, every ocean bar the Atlantic was under enemy control, continental Europe was overrun by German troops, and the British Army had enjoyed no lasting success anywhere on the globe.

Churchill gave a powerful defence of his administration in Parliament and secured an overwhelming majority in his favour, but even he became shaken over the next few weeks as bad news continued to pour into the Map Room. There were reverses for British troops in North Africa, and almost continual losses of territory in the Far East, with the fall of Singapore on 15 February a desperate low point. To make matters worse, the number of merchant ships being lost to Nazi submarines was getting higher and higher. Churchill later admitted that this 'U-boat peril' was the one thing that really frightened him. It is all too easy to imagine him staring in concern at the vast convoy map that dominates one wall of the Map Room and worrying about whether Britain would soon lack the capacity to stay in the war.

Since the fall of France in 1940, the only way that Britain could strike back directly at Germany was from the air, but by early 1942 it was becoming clear that the RAF's bombers did not have either the range or the accuracy to inflict serious strategic damage. Many parts of Germany were out of reach and only one in four bombs fell within five miles of its target. Behind the scenes at the War Rooms, and tabled for discussion by the Chiefs of Staff and the War Cabinet, the question was raised of how to go about exacting a more effective strategic return. The result was a decision to switch to 'area bombing', subjecting broad swathes of German cities to concentrated – and controversial – attack.

While the RAF was engaged in these deadly operations, the British Army was struggling to stand its ground in the Far East and in North Africa. News of fresh defeats and humiliations came so regularly that Churchill began to doubt whether the troops were up to the job – a fear shared by Alan Brooke, who had become the Army Chief of Staff at the end of 1941. 'If the Army cannot fight better than it is doing at present,' Brooke confided in his diary, 'we shall deserve to lose our Empire.'

The Army's performance proved especially embarrassing to Churchill during his second visit to Washington in June 1942. During one meeting in the Oval Office he was handed news of the fall of Tobruk to German troops in North Africa – news made all the more difficult to take coming, as it did, in front of Roosevelt himself. Once more Churchill found himself returning to Britain with his own future at risk. 'Now for England,' he said as he departed Washington, 'home, and a beautiful row.'

This time Parliament was debating a vote of censure about the Prime Minister's conduct of the war. He survived the vote 475 to 25, but was sorely wounded by the many critical comments made during the debate. Knowing that he needed to reverse the tide of events, Churchill took to his travels again that August, flying to Cairo, Moscow and Teheran to do whatever he could to influence the war on the ground. It was in Cairo that he decided to shake up command of the Army in North Africa, bringing in a new Commander-in-Chief, General Harold Alexander, and a new Commander of the Eighth Army, Lieutenant General William Gott.

Tragically, Gott was killed when the plane carrying him to Cairo was shot down – a reminder of the dangers facing Churchill himself on his many travels. Casting around for a suitable replacement, Churchill was persuaded by Brooke to select General Bernard Montgomery. It would prove to be an inspired decision. During the last days of October and early November 1942, British troops under Montgomery's command fought a fierce battle near the town of El Alamein and secured a significant victory. Back in London, Churchill was quick to seize upon the moment with a typical rhetorical flourish: 'This is not the end. It is not even the beginning of the end. But it is, perhaps, the end of the beginning.'

The success at El Alamein and the almost unopposed Allied landings in North Africa on 8 November marked a turning point in the war. After three long

Montgomery watches the beginning of the German retreat from El Alamein from the turret of his Grant Tank, 5 November 1942

Winston Churchill stands on the battlement of the Citadel in Quebec during the Quebec Conference, Canada, August 1943

the utmost secrecy to house a secure radio-telephone link between the Prime Minister and the President of the United States. The equipment in this Transatlantic Telephone Room – and a huge scrambling unit stored beneath Selfridges department store – made it impossible for the Germans to listen in to or decipher any conversation between the two leaders.

The hotline between London and Washington became operational in August 1943, at which point Churchill was in Quebec holding talks with the President in person. It was at the Quebec conference that a date was finally set for the invasion of north-west France. Churchill was still far from sure that this was the correct strategy, but in the months since Casablanca the US had become the more senior partner on the ground in Europe and British influence on events was waning. The date set for the landings was May 1944. Back in the War Rooms, preparations for Operation Overlord shifted up several gears. D-Day was approaching.

THE
CHURCHILL
SUITE

Early in 1941, as the Blitz raged on, the Cabinet War Rooms were expanded to include rooms for the private use of the Prime Minister and his wife. As it turned out, the worst of the bombing raids had passed by the time the rooms were ready, and little is known about how often they were used – if at all – for the remainder of the war. When in London, the Prime Minister and Mrs Churchill preferred to live in the No 10 Annexe – a set of rooms reserved for them in the building above the War Rooms.

After the war, this section of the War Rooms was stripped out and fell into disrepair. Its restoration required a combination of ingenuity and persistence from IWM's staff.

The sink, sump and pump displayed in the kitchen were found in a neglected corner of the Treasury Building. The hand-operated pump was used to remove waste water and force it back up to surface level (the underground kitchen had to operate without proper plumbing or gas).

◀ The decision to create a suite of rooms underground for the Churchills was prompted when a bomb on 14 October 1940 destroyed the kitchen at 10 Downing Street. Just moments before the blast, Churchill had been standing in the kitchen persuading his chef, Georgina Landemare, to take shelter in the building's basement. Mrs Landemare duly survived the blast and would go on to make use of this new kitchen in the War Rooms as well as one in the No 10 Annexe. A number of the pots, pans and utensils in the kitchen were given to the museum by the granddaughter of Mrs Landemare. Churchill's cook had been allowed to keep them when she retired from their service in 1954 at the age of 72.

▼ For more than forty years the sign for Clementine Churchill's room was in the possession of American serviceman Lieutenant Ray Edghill. It was Edghill's job to set up the connection in the Transatlantic Telephone Room whenever a call was scheduled between Churchill and the US President. During one visit to the War Rooms in 1945, the American noticed the plaque sticking up out of a bin and decided to save it for posterity. In the months before the museum was opened in 1984, he contacted IWM and arranged for it to be returned.

Mary Churchill pictured with her father onboard HMS *Duke of York*, December 1941.

MARY CHURCHILL'S EXPERIENCE

The Prime Minister's daugher, Mary Churchill, sometimes made use of her mother's bedroom in the War Rooms when on leave from the Auxiliary Territorial Service. It is not an experience that she remembered fondly:

'When I stayed I was allotted one of the emergency bedrooms in the Cabinet War Rooms complex down below the Annexe flat; my clothes, however, were kept (mostly in my suitcase) in a bathroom used by the women secretaries (which cannot have been convenient for them). At night, I would get into my nightclothes there and make my way 'down below'. Passing the sentry on duty at the Annexe front door on my way up and down in my dressing gown and tin hat was a perpetual source of humiliation to me, as I imagined he must think I was the only 'windy' one in the family!'

▼ Mrs Churchill's room is notable for the absence of a desk and the apparent attempts to soften the spartan accommodation with items such as an armchair, with its softer fabric and upholstery. It is unlikely that Mrs Churchill herself had any hand in the layout of the room, but she did take a guiding interest in the furnishing of the No 10 Annexe above, painting the walls, hanging pictures and using much of the couple's own furniture. Her husband couldn't see the point of taking such trouble, but he later admitted that she had done a good job.

▶ A set of photographs of the War Rooms taken in 1946, including this one of Mrs Churchill's bedroom, later proved vital to the restoration process. In 1983 IWM's curators also discovered a box of objects from Mrs Churchill's bedroom that had remained unopened since the war. The sheets and pillowcases that it contained had disintegrated, but the black Bakelite telephone and white porcelain water jugs had survived and have since been restored to their old positions.

It is unlikely that the Churchills ever ate a meal in the dining room reserved for their use. It is arguably the most incongruous room in the whole underground complex, with its well-appointed furniture standing in contrast to the whitewashed brick walls.

The table and sideboard in the dining room are the originals that furnished the room in wartime.

CHURCHILL'S ENTOURAGE

When the corridor that leads to the Churchill Suite was opened up in spring 1941, several other rooms were also made available for use. Some were assigned to members of Churchill's personal staff, such as his bodyguards, his aide-de-camp Commander Charles 'Tommy' Thompson, his Parliamentary Private Secretary Brigadier George Harvie-Watt, and the head of his secretarial pool Margaret Stenhouse. Others were given to key members of his inner circle, such as his intelligence adviser Major Desmond Morton and his close friend and Minister of Information Brendan Bracken. Some of these rooms have been restored for viewing today.

Brendan Bracken was one of Churchill's closest confidants. A fellow Conservative MP, he acted as Churchill's Parliamentary Private Secretary until 1941, when he was appointed Minister of Information – a role he carried out with great success. This set of pyjamas is on display in Bracken's room. Like Desmond Morton and Churchill's scientific adviser Frederick Lindemann, Bracken was unmarried and had plenty of time to devote to the Prime Minister. In Bracken's case, this does not seem to have endeared him to Mrs Churchill, who is said to have mistrusted his influence on her husband.

Naval officer Commander Charles 'Tommy' Thompson was the Prime Minister's aide-de-camp – a kind of military personal assistant. He was rarely seen away from Churchill's side during the war, so it is no surprise that he was given emergency accommodation in the War Rooms (shown above is a razor on display in Thompson's room). One of Thompson's duties involved making travel arrangements for Churchill's entourage and baggage – this was no mean feat considering how unpredictable Churchill's movements could be.

It is unknown how often – if at all – Commander Thompson made use of his underground bedroom/ study. Given the Prime Minister's preference for staying above ground, it is likely that Thompson chose to do the same.

This asbestos cloth dispenser and the nearby boxes of anti-louse powder are the same as were actually present in this room in August 1945.

The bell displayed on the wall was found in another government building and added to the room during its restoration. It is actually a division bell, one of hundreds in the buildings immediately around Parliament, which were used to alert MPs whenever a vote was imminent.

As Prime Minister, Churchill was given a two-man Special Branch protection team. The senior of the two bodyguards was Detective Walter H Thompson, who had been assigned to protect Churchill between 1921 and 1935 before retiring in 1936. On 22 August 1939 Thompson was working in the family grocer's shop when he received a telegram from Churchill. 'Meet me Croydon Airport 4.30pm Wednesday,' it read. Thompson was back on the job.

The room for Churchill's detectives was fitted with bunk-beds to accommodate the two men who alternated on bodyguard duty. A stretcher was on stand-by to carry the Prime Minister in case he was injured in the War Rooms.

After the war, Walter Thompson revealed that Churchill was determined to go down fighting. Thompson was ordered to keep a .45 Colt pistol fully loaded for the Prime Minister's use. 'He intended to use every bullet but one on the enemy,' wrote the detective. 'The last one he saved for himself.'

Churchill is seen with Detective Thompson, August 1940

A RELUCTANT GUEST

After the war Thompson wrote an account of his time as the Prime Minister's bodyguard. Here he recalls how hard it was to persuade Churchill to stay overnight in the War Rooms:

'Mrs Churchill made him promise to go down below when the raid started, and requested me to see that he carried out her wishes... I was mystified by the docility with which he went downstairs and noticed with some apprehension the cynical smile on his face...

' "Leave [the light] on, Thompson", said the Old Man. I retired to my own room, but I did not undress. Sure enough, not long afterwards, Mr Churchill rang his bell... He had put on a dressing gown and was gathering up his papers. "Well, Thompson, I have kept my word," he said with a chuckle. "I came downstairs to go to bed. Now I am going upstairs to sleep!" '

During the inter-war years, Major Desmond Morton worked in military intelligence – thanks to the intervention of Churchill, when he was Secretary of State for War between 1919 and 1922. In the 1930s, when Churchill was out of favour, Morton became a valued member of his inner circle, keeping him in the loop on military and intelligence matters. It was a role he would continue to fulfil on a more official basis during the war.

There were no washing facilities available at basement level, so each bedroom contained a washing jug and bowl for the occupant's use. Seen here are those on display in Major Morton's room.

SWITCHBOARD

Many of the rooms in Churchill's bunker performed a variety of roles during the war. Room 60 Right was originally used by typists before serving as a switchboard from the summer of 1940 through to at least spring 1941. Later in the war, as more space became available elsewhere in the basement, it was reserved as emergency accommodation, and by the end of the war it had become an office for the Royal Marine guards. Today it has been restored to reflect the role that it carried out as home to the War Rooms switchboard.

Switchboard operators in the War Rooms – and at places like the Post Office, hospitals and airfields – were given specially adapted gas masks that would allow them to continue their work even in the event of a gas attack. Fortunately they were only ever put to use in drills.

Throughout the darkest days of the Blitz, shifts of switchboard operators would work, two at a time, in this room at all hours of the day and night. It was their job to connect the War Rooms to the outside world.

Until the spring of 1941 space in the War Rooms was extremely hard to come by, meaning that two or three typists were also crammed in beside the switchboard operators. It was only when the protective concrete slab was expanded to cover more of the basement rooms that the pressure eased. One of the new rooms became a new, and much bigger, switchboard facility.

TYPISTS

From July 1940 to July 1941, Room 60A was occupied by the typing pool for the Joint Planning Staff. It was later partitioned to form two smaller emergency bedrooms, but has now been restored to reflect the period of the war in which it saw the most sustained activity.

Each typist worked beneath a green-shaded lamp slung low from the ceiling. When interviewed by IWM historians during the restoration of the War Rooms one of the typists, Margaret d'Arcy (née Sutherland), described how they would sometimes stick paper over the underside of the lamps to reduce the intensity of the light.

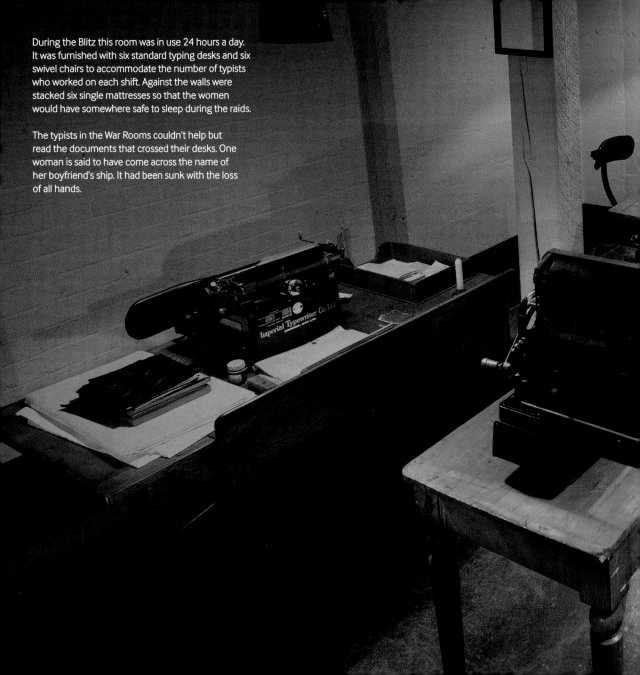

During the Blitz this room was in use 24 hours a day. It was furnished with six standard typing desks and six swivel chairs to accommodate the number of typists who worked on each shift. Against the walls were stacked six single mattresses so that the women would have somewhere safe to sleep during the raids.

The typists in the War Rooms couldn't help but read the documents that crossed their desks. One woman is said to have come across the name of her boyfriend's ship. It had been sunk with the loss of all hands.

OFFICES OF THE WAR CABINET

GREAT GEORGE STREET, S.W.1

Reference No.
1/G/1095

20th July, 1943.

Dear Madam,

I am authorised, subject to satisfactory references being received, to offer you an appointment as a Temporary Shorthand Typist Grade II in this Office; and subject to one month's probation.

The wages attached to the post are 47/- plus 13/6 war bonus per week, for a minimum attendance of 44 hours per week, and are subject to statutory deductions in respect of National Health and Unemployment Insurance.

Sick and Annual Leave are authorised in accordance with the attached statement.

The appointment will be a temporary one for the war period, subject to one week's notice in writing on either side.

If you are willing to accept this appointment will you please let me know, and report to me at the above address, ready to commence your duties, at 9.30 a.m. on Monday, 26th July, 1943.

Yours faithfully,

[signature]

Chief Clerk.

▲ Demand for administrative support at the War Rooms was always high, meaning that letters like this one were probably sent out quite frequently. This rare surviving example is lodged in IWM's archives.

▶ When more copies of a document were needed, a stencil was prepared for use in a Gestetner copier like this one. The stencil was put in place, the ink readied and paper was wound through the machine using a hand-operated crank. It was a laborious but essential process.

◀ It was the job of the typing pool to produce accurate versions of all the handwritten minutes and reports generated by the Joint Planning Staff. They worked using Imperial typewriters like this one, producing one top copy and two carbon copies of each sheet.

THE TRANSATLANTIC
TELEPHONE ROOM

In the first few years of the war, transatlantic conversations
between the Prime Minister and the US President were
conducted via a radio-telephone link known to be vulnerable
to enemy eavesdropping. To ensure secrecy, censors had
to be employed to listen in to every conversation and cut
the line whenever a forbidden subject was mentioned.
In the summer of 1943, it was agreed that a new system
should be used, which would encrypt the conversation so
that it could no longer be deciphered by enemy spies. Work
duly began to transform a store cupboard in the War Rooms
to become one end of this top secret hotline.

The system used for the transatlantic telephone link was
designed by Bell Telephone Laboratories in the US. Codenamed
'Sigsaly' and sometimes referred to as the 'X system' or 'X-Ray',
it was considered so valuable by the Americans that they were
reluctant to share any of its workings with the British. In the
end it was agreed that the machinery should be checked for its
effectiveness by British codebreaking pioneer Alan Turing. Once
he gave his blessing, work began in earnest and the system was
ready for use by Churchill from August 1943.

CIGARETTE
ENDS.

◀ The clock in the telephone room sported two black hands to indicate London time, and two red ones to show the equivalent time in Washington. According to the stipulations of the Americans, calls had to be pre-booked an hour in advance and could only be made between the hours of 2pm and 8pm. This was hardly designed to fit in comfortably with the peculiarities of Churchill's daily schedule, so it is perhaps unsurprising that he did not make use of the system until April 1944.

▶ Churchill's Personal Secretary used this headset to listen in to the conversation in order to take notes. The presence of two people in the narrow confines of the room must have added to its claustrophobic atmosphere.

◀ Sigsaly was designed to allow senior US personnel to talk in secrecy between the UK and the USA. The machinery required to make it work was installed in three large rooms below Selfridges department store in the West End. When it was decided to extend this capability to the War Rooms, a cable was run from Selfridges to this small intermediate scrambling machine in the corner of the Transatlantic Telephone Room.

When Churchill spoke into the ordinary looking phone handset, his words were immediately scrambled by the machine in the corner of the room. This partially enciphered signal was then transmitted to the Selfridges machinery, where it was fully enciphered and sent by radio to Washington. There it was received and decoded by the same equipment.

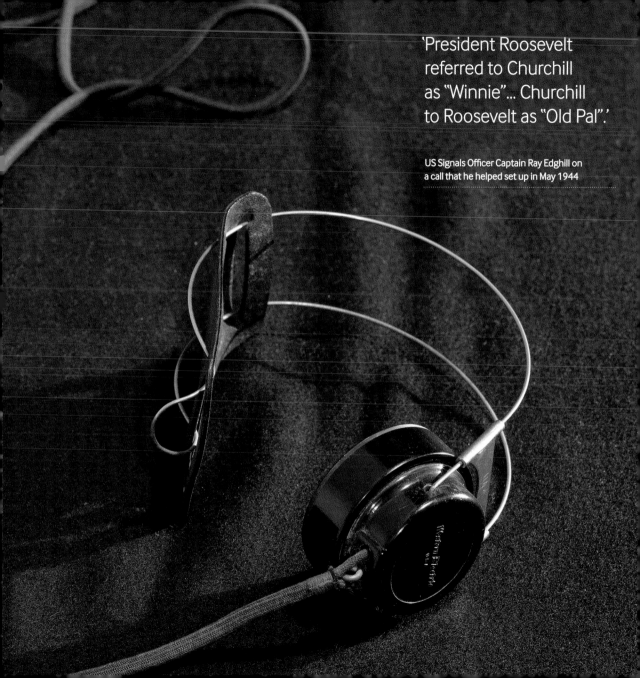

'President Roosevelt referred to Churchill as "Winnie"... Churchill to Roosevelt as "Old Pal".'

US Signals Officer Captain Ray Edghill on a call that he helped set up in May 1944

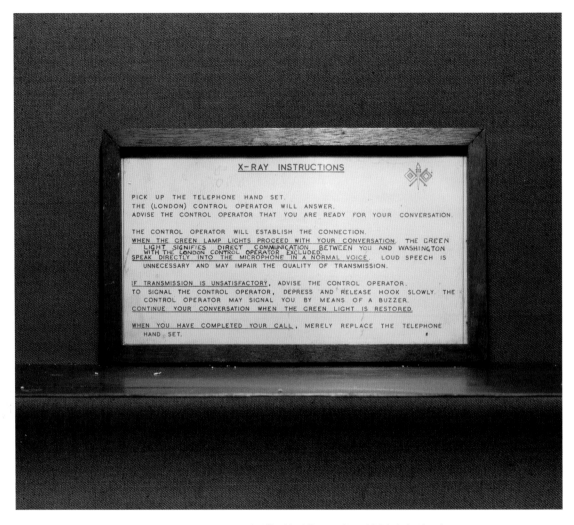

X-RAY INSTRUCTIONS

PICK UP THE TELEPHONE HAND SET.
THE (LONDON) CONTROL OPERATOR WILL ANSWER.
ADVISE THE CONTROL OPERATOR THAT YOU ARE READY FOR YOUR CONVERSATION.

THE CONTROL OPERATOR WILL ESTABLISH THE CONNECTION.
WHEN THE GREEN LAMP LIGHTS PROCEED WITH YOUR CONVERSATION. THE GREEN
  LIGHT SIGNIFIES DIRECT COMMUNICATION BETWEEN YOU AND WASHINGTON
  WITH THE LONDON CONTROL OPERATOR EXCLUDED.
SPEAK DIRECTLY INTO THE MICROPHONE IN A NORMAL VOICE. LOUD SPEECH IS
  UNNECESSARY AND MAY IMPAIR THE QUALITY OF TRANSMISSION.

IF TRANSMISSION IS UNSATISFACTORY, ADVISE THE CONTROL OPERATOR.
TO SIGNAL THE CONTROL OPERATOR, DEPRESS AND RELEASE HOOK SLOWLY. THE
  CONTROL OPERATOR MAY SIGNAL YOU BY MEANS OF A BUZZER.
CONTINUE YOUR CONVERSATION WHEN THE GREEN LIGHT IS RESTORED.

WHEN YOU HAVE COMPLETED YOUR CALL, MERELY REPLACE THE TELEPHONE
  HAND SET.

▲ The frame above the desk contains a set of 'X-Ray Instructions', including a warning that shouting down the phone line was likely to impair the quality of transmission. The system could have other peculiar effects on a person's voice. On one occasion, it is said that President Roosevelt couldn't help but laugh on hearing Churchill speak down the line. Apparently the bulldog British Prime Minister sounded remarkably like cartoon character Donald Duck.

▲ Only a few of the War Rooms staff were aware of the plans to create the Transatlantic Telephone Room. All they knew was that an old store cupboard was being readied for some new purpose. When a new door was fitted, complete with a lavatory-style lock, the purpose appeared to become clear – Churchill must have been given the luxury of his own private flushing toilet.

4

THE
FINAL PUSH

January 1944 to August 1945

In spring 1944 Prime Minister Winston Churchill set aside his misgivings about the invasion of north-west France. He threw himself into the preparations, involving himself deeply in the work of the many Joint Planning and Joint Intelligence committees set up in the War Rooms to cover every aspect of the operation. He was characteristically interested in some of the more ingenious aspects of the landings: the floating Mulberry Harbours designed to transform the beaches into efficient entry points for troops and materiel; the deception schemes employed to divert German attention from the landing sites; and the series of modified armoured vehicles, known as 'funnies', that saw ordinary tanks become beach-combing minesweepers or flame-throwers.

As this work continued, London once more became subject to bombing raids in a 'Little Blitz' that began on 21 January and continued sporadically until 19 April. On 20 February bombs fell just yards away from the War Rooms, hitting Horse Guards Parade and St James's Park and causing damage to 10 Downing Street. Writing about the raids in his diary, Churchill's private secretary John Colville noted that London seemed to react with less ebullience than it had in 1940 and 1941. Churchill too seems to have struggled during this period, with Alan Brooke describing him as 'losing ground rapidly' and 'desperately tired' following a Chiefs of Staff meeting in March. But far from being the cause of the Prime Minister's travails, the bombing raids seem almost to have had an energising effect on him. One of the officers in the No 10 Annexe remembers how he would 'have his coat and tin hat got ready so that as soon as the guns opened fire he might proceed to the roof of the building to get a better view'.

Always keen to show off his underground facility, Churchill invited the US Chiefs of Staff and General Eisenhower – the Supreme Commander of the Allied forces – to meet with him in the War Rooms.

The Map Room was of course the highlight of the tour, while Churchill's bedroom study next door provided somewhere more informal to sit after a lengthy conference. In April the Prime Minister also made use of the Transatlantic Telephone Room for the first time – as US telecommunications engineer Stephen Geis described many years later in conversation with IWM historians. Geis recalls that he stopped on his way to the War Rooms to buy the best cigar he could in case he met Churchill in person. 'Sure enough the Prime Minister, dressed in his boiler suit, came in… He took the cigar and I stepped outside… It was the thrill of my military experience.'

Throughout this period the date set for the landings was, of course, a fiercely guarded secret but it was one necessarily known to many of the staff at the War Rooms, from the officers planning the operation to the stenographers and typists beavering away on all the associated reports, minutes and briefing papers. 'Many of us knew the date of "D-Day" from the hour "Operation Overlord" was first mentioned,' said Joan Bright, who was personal assistant to General Ismay. The need for secrecy was hammered home to all staff early in the war, with one shorthand typist remembering how a colleague was led away in tears by two men she assumed were detectives. It was a message that seems to have got through, with many former staff concealing their wartime activities even from their families for decades to come.

One especially well-kept secret was Churchill's desire to be present in person at the D-Day landings – which had now been put back to the first week of June. Towards the end of May the Prime Minister informed the Admiralty that he intended to witness the operation first-hand from the decks of HMS *Belfast* – the cruiser given the honour of firing the opening shots of D-Day (now a branch of IWM moored on the Thames). The idea of Britain's wartime leader placing himself in such danger was quite clearly preposterous, but it wasn't until King George VI intervened in two separate letters – the second dated as late as 4 June – that Churchill agreed to back down.

Two days later at 5.27am HMS *Belfast* duly began bombarding one of the beaches chosen for the landings – although another trigger-happy ship stole the honour of the first shot by about a minute. Churchill eventually made it to the Normandy coast on board the destroyer HMS *Kelvin* on 12 June, and made sure that the ship joined in with the bombardment of German positions while he was on the bridge. By that stage Allied troops had secured a firm foothold along the coastline and the scene was set for a bitter struggle south and eastwards towards Germany.

Churchill was back in London on 13 June – in time to receive reports of 'flying bombs' appearing in the skies above south-east England. This was the first use by Germany of its *Vergeltungswaffen* or 'revenge weapons', and as wave after wave of 'V1s' continued to swarm over the Channel at any hour of the day or night, the staff of the War Rooms were once more glad of the protection afforded by their underground location. Five days later David Lee, an officer in the Joint Planning section, was working at his desk when the monotonous thrum of the ventilation fans was suddenly shattered.

It was a Sunday morning…and at eleven o'clock there was an appalling explosion. We were working down there in our office and our first thought was that we'd been hit. Well, it was the bomb that fell on the Guards Chapel about two to three hundred yards down Birdcage Walk in the middle of the morning service. A lot of people were killed and what happened was the force of the explosion travelled underground and rocked us about. It didn't do any damage – we were too far away – but I remember that incident very well.

The next day the meeting of the War Cabinet was held in the shelter of the War Rooms for the first time that year. It would become a regular haunt for Churchill, his ministers and his Chiefs of Staff throughout the rest of June, July and August, until 9 September when the threat posed by the V1s began to dwindle in the face of more effective defence measures.

By this stage, the walls of the Map Room were showing US troops on the western border of Germany, Soviet troops advancing into German territory in the east and a newly liberated Paris back in the hands of the Free French forces. Churchill, meanwhile, was in Quebec for a second bilateral conference with the Americans. Little of note was achieved at the meeting, where both sides appeared to steer clear of their strategic differences. The Americans were content to spend time massing their troops ahead of what they hoped would be a decisive offensive against the centre of the German lines. The British, on the other hand, were keen to push into Germany quickly so that they could meet the Russian forces as far east as possible and so limit the advance of Communism across the Continent.

Churchill returned to Britain on 26 September, by which time London was facing a new threat in the form of the V2 rocket – the world's first ballistic missile. Intelligence reports about these deadly new weapons had started to filter through to the War Rooms in 1943, and they were on the agenda at both meetings of the War Cabinet held underground that year. Concern about their destructive potential led to renewed calls for the War Rooms to be moved away from the capital, but Churchill once more refused to budge unless London suffered a scale of attack far worse than anything experienced to date.

The number of V2 rockets launched against London steadily increased, until on 9 January 1945 the War Cabinet was once more forced to meet underground. There it would largely stay until 28 March, when most of the V2 launching sites had been overrun by the advancing Allied forces. That meeting of the War Cabinet was the 115th to be held underground during the war – out of a total of 1,188 held between September 1939 and July 1945. It also turned out to be the last.

Much of the attention of the War Cabinet at this time was focussed on the shape of the post-war world. This too was the main subject for discussion by the 'Big Three' – Churchill, Roosevelt and Stalin – at the Yalta Conference held in February 1945. Some 750 ministers, officers and support staff set out from London for the Crimea. Most travelled by ship but the Prime Minister, Chiefs of Staff and senior officers went by three planes that took off from RAF Northolt on 29 January. Only two of the planes, including the one carrying Churchill, made it to the stop-off point on Malta. The third overshot the island and crashed into the sea, killing 14 of the 19 passengers on-board. It was shocking news for the close-knit community of the War Rooms, where several of the victims, including one Map Room officer, were well known. It was also another grim reminder of the dangers that Churchill faced on his many wartime journeys.

The Yalta Conference itself turned out to be a gloomy affair for the British delegation, which once again found itself sidelined by the two larger superpowers. Churchill himself couldn't wait to leave, stopping off in Athens, Alexandria and Cairo before flying home on what would be his last long-distance journey of the war. It was also the last time he would see President Roosevelt, who died after a prolonged decline in health on 12 April.

London in April 1945 was a city transformed. The terrors of the V-weapon offensive were over, and when staff emerged from the War Rooms at the end of a long day's shift they were greeted by street lamps lit for the first time in five years. Berlin, in contrast, was a city on the verge of ruin. Hitler was locked in his own bunker, trapped by bombing raids and Allied armies converging from east and west. It was a complex originally designed as a temporary air raid shelter for the Führer, but expanded during the war to include facilities such as a Map Room, bedrooms, offices and switchboard. It was here in his study that Hitler committed suicide on 30 April.

Just over a week later, on 8 May, the Allies declared Victory in Europe Day, sparking huge celebrations in central London. Shorthand typist Ilene Hutchinson remembers how she and other War Rooms staff climbed on to the rooftop to see what was going on:

> We got up onto the roof of the office and we managed to walk right along to... the Home Office, I think, but on the roof... We watched all the crowds, thousands and thousands and thousands. There was hardly a hair's breadth between them. They just held hands... and it was amazing. And then, when Mr Churchill appeared in this open limousine, he had his hat in one hand, cigar in the other and he was just standing waving them both and of course they went mad. Absolute frenzy there was... Then I had to go back to work!

Before this early evening appearance in Whitehall, Churchill had lunched with the King, delivered a broadcast to the nation, spoken in the House of Commons, attended a service of thanksgiving, spent an hour in the smoking room at Parliament and then returned to Buckingham Palace with the War Cabinet and Chiefs of Staff for royal congratulations. It was a day of great public celebration, but in private his morale was low. The war against Japan still needed to be won, the shape of post-war Europe was in the balance, Britain's coffers were empty and serious cracks were beginning to appear in his coalition government. He took to spending much more time 'working in bed', and became so infirm that he had to be carried up and down to the War Rooms on a wooden chair by the Royal Marines.

His visits to the War Rooms were now solely made to use the Transatlantic Telephone Room and to drop into the Map Room to catch up with progress in the war against Japan. The other rooms in the underground complex were already being vacated – with staff no longer needing the protection of a concrete slab and steel girders above their heads. Even for those left behind, including the Joint Planners working on the continuing war in the Far East, thoughts were beginning to turn to life after the war – to new careers, relationships and homes.

Churchill's position in the post-war world was also uncertain. He had hoped to hold his coalition government together until Japan was defeated, but the Labour Party disagreed. By 12 June, the Prime Minister bowed to the inevitable. Parliament was dissolved and a general election – the first in a decade – was set for 5 July. Churchill fought a vigorous campaign and, when the polls closed, he was confident of victory. The result, however, would not be announced until 26 July to allow time for millions of votes to come in from troops stationed abroad.

In the meantime, Churchill was able to take a short holiday in the south of France before his attention switched to the Potsdam Conference scheduled for 17 July. The city of Potsdam lies just outside Berlin, so the trip to Germany gave Churchill and his entourage the chance to visit the capital of the ruined Third Reich. Dressed in military uniform, the British leader picked his way through the rubble above Hitler's bunker. Perhaps his mind went back to the words he growled out almost five years earlier, on the day he first entered his own War Rooms as Prime Minister: 'If the invasion takes place,' he had said, 'that's where I'll sit – in that chair. And I'll sit there until either the Germans are driven back – or they carry me out dead.' How the tables had been turned.

Many of Churchill's staff also found their thoughts wandering. Amid the euphoria of victory came a depression so commonly felt that it was given its own name – the Potsdam Blues. For some the trigger was the sight of defeated Germans in 'pathetic groups trudging wearily along in search of wood for fuel'. For others it was the smell of 'decayed death' that seemed to permeate the bombed out ruins. There was also a growing understanding that an extraordinary passage of their lives was closing. Securing victory was merely the turning of the page to a new and undoubtedly much less exciting chapter.

A few days into the conference, Churchill flew back to be on the spot for the announcement of the election result, a little less sure of the outcome than he had been just weeks earlier. Few among his entourage saw anything to worry about; one was confident enough to leave most of his baggage behind in the expectation of a swift return. He was soon making arrangements to have it sent back. Labour had won a landslide victory; the electorate deciding that the country's social problems required a more progressive set of solutions than the Conservatives could offer.

Churchill was disconsolate, spending the day of the announcement locked away in the No 10 Annexe above the War Rooms. He emerged shortly before 7 o'clock in the evening to go to Buckingham Palace to tender his resignation. The following day he bid a succession of farewells to the Cabinet, his Chiefs of Staff and to the many men and women who had served him so faithfully above and below ground in that anonymous building on Great George Street. Alan Brooke, the army chief with whom Churchill had

Winston Churchill makes a speech in Uxbridge, Middlesex, during
the general election campaign, 27 June 1945

clashed so often throughout the war, later wrote in his diary: 'It was a very sad and very moving little meeting at which I found myself unable to say much for fear of breaking down.' He ended with an encomium to the outgoing leader: 'I thank God that I was given an opportunity of working alongside of such a man, and of having my eyes opened to the fact that occasionally such supermen exist on this earth.'

As these scenes played out in the No 10 Annexe, the staff in the War Rooms continued to update their maps, plotting out the gains of territory across the Pacific, and the bombing raids over the Japanese mainland. But even in the Map Room, officers were beginning to move on. On 3 August, Ismay, who had set the creation of the War Rooms in motion, told Wing Commander John Heagerty, one of the Map Room duty officers: 'It is very sad to realise that my old friends in the Map Room are leaving one by one, and that what was once a haunt of intense interest and great friendliness will be merely an empty shell.'

In the coming days the phones in the Map Room rang to bring news of the atom bombs dropped over Hiroshima and Nagasaki. Then came talk of a Japanese surrender, which duly came on 14 August. The following day, the officers on duty in the Map Room gathered up their possessions, exchanged congratulations and made ready to head out into the summer sunshine. The last man to leave paused at the door and reached for a switch. For the first time in six years, the lights in the Map Room were turned off. The war was over.

EVERYDAY
LIFE

Everywhere you look in the War Rooms, there are details that hint at what daily life must have been like here in wartime. Almost all staff worked in shifts, but were often required to stay at their desks well beyond their appointed hours. The officers had their own mess in what is now the museum shop, but would also eat at their clubs above ground. Other staff would also eat out at nearby cafes if possible but, after spring 1942, they could choose to eat at a canteen set up for them in a more distant part of the basement. Between shifts, staff could make their way home or make use of their accommodation – the lucky ones in private rooms on the basement level, the rest in dormitories a floor further down.

▲ The busy staff of the War Rooms were afforded their own post box for sending out personal correspondence. It was emptied four times a day. Staff walking down the main corridor could also check to see if they had received any personal mail.

Lieutenant General Sir Leslie Hollis, c.1947

SECRECY

As Senior Assistant Secretary to the War Cabinet, Lieutenant General Sir Leslie Hollis was privy to all kinds of top secret information. Keeping it secret could be difficult and frustrating, as he explains in this extract from his memoirs:

'Outside the office, one was reluctant to talk about the war to anyone, however prominent or well-known. I remember travelling to my home in Sussex to see for a few hours my wife when she was ill. In the train there was one other civilian gentleman in the compartment. I was in uniform and the civilian started a conversation about the course of the war. His questions were very much to the point and I knew most of the answers, but in every case I pleaded complete ignorance. As I got off the train he gave me a withering look of contempt, as much as to say: "No wonder we are doing so badly when such flannelled fools are allowed to hold the King's Commission!"'

▶ In the summer of 1938 George Rance had been an Office of Works official, less than a year away from retirement. Over the following months he became integral to the development and everyday running of the War Rooms. To maintain secrecy, for example, all the furniture, maps and documents required to equip the site were addressed simply 'c/o Mr Rance, Office of Works, Whitehall'. During the war the Grenadier Guards protecting the War Rooms were nicknamed 'Rance's Guard'. After the war, Rance continued to watch over the site and he acted as an unofficial guide to interested parties. Here he is seen adjusting the weather indicator board – the only means by which staff could know what conditions to expect above ground.

▼ Churchill is credited with the invention of this label, which was used to mark the most urgent documents in circulation.

▼ In the interests of economy, lights were expected to be turned off whenever a room was not in use.

NOTICE

TURN OFF THAT SWITCH PLEASE:—

THIS DOCUMENT IS THE PROPERTY OF HIS BRITANNIC MAJESTY'S GOVERNMENT

The circulation of this paper has been strictly limited.

It is issued for the personal use of..................................

TOP
~~MOST~~ SECRET.   Copy No............

MOST SECRET ~ TO BE BURNT BEFORE READING

J.P.(T)(42) 1. (FINAL)

9th May 1942

WAR CABINET

JOINT PLANNING TYPISTS

OPERATION "DESPERATE"

Report by the J.P. Typing Pool

In view of the recent changes in the Government policy
of distribution of coupons,* we have examined the situation,
and the following conclusions have been reached:-

    (a) The limitation of supplies in the U.K. has resulted
        in the following acute shortages -

          (i) silk stockings;
          (ii) chocolates;
          (iii) cosmetics.

    (b) The lack of these vital commodities is regarded as
        extremely serious and may, in consequence, become
        a source of extreme embarrassment. This must be
        avoided at all costs.

    (c) It is felt that immediate steps should be taken to
        explore the possibilities of U.S. resources.

2.   In the light of the above, it is considered that the most
expedient method of implementing the proposal in (c) would be
the early despatch of a mission to the U.S.A; a Force Commander
has already been appointed, in anticipation of instructions.
    Accordingly, we attach a draft directive♪ to the officer
concerned.

            (Signed) NAUSEA D. BAGWASH
                      LIZZI LIGHT-ffOOT
                      MAGGIE DEUCE
                      DEADLY NIGHTSHADE
                      JUNE WINTERBOTTHAM (Mrs)

  * As from May 31st - only 60 in 14 months!
  ♪ Annex

-1-

◄ In May 1942 – ahead of Churchill's second visit to Washington – some of the female staff in the War Rooms produced this light-hearted memorandum on the subject of Operation 'Desperate'. The mission it describes, which gives an insight into the dreary conditions endured by Britons during the war, is said to have been a complete success.

► To alleviate the health problems associated with working underground for prolonged periods of time, staff were made to strip to their underwear, put on a pair of protective goggles and stand in front of portable sun lamps like this one. Incidences of 'sunburn' were common, and one veteran recalls a 'silly girl' who forgot to put on the goggles and nearly went blind.

'We started with one minute each side and got up to probably ten minutes. I remember, being fair skinned, sometimes I would be as red as a beetroot.'

Leading Aircraftwoman Myra Murden on using the Sol Tan box

Operating Instructions

for

SOL-TAN

HIGH PRESSURE MERCURY
ARC ULTRA-VIOLET LAMPS

Nos. EM/96P, 97P, 98P, 99P, 365P,
415P, 415P/FM, 415/36P

THE CHIEFS OF STAFF
CONFERENCE ROOM

In spring 1941 the expansion of the protective concrete slab above the War Rooms made another section of the basement available for use. By late July this large room was set aside as a reserve conference room for the Chiefs of Staff – the heads of the Army, Navy and Air Force. Most of the time the Chiefs would hold their meetings on the second floor of the building above the War Rooms, but they would often come down here during the V-weapon offensives in 1944 and 1945.

By the time of the V-weapon offensives, the Chiefs of Staff were Admiral of the Fleet Sir Andrew Cunningham, Air Chief Marshal Sir Charles Portal and General Sir Alan Brooke. The decisions that they made in this 'New Map Room' determined the movements of hundreds of thousands of military personnel across the globe.

'This is the powerhouse of war...
these great men sitting there at
the table. It was deeply moving.'

Alan Melville, a member of the Joint Planning Staff,
on once attending a Chiefs of Staff meeting

◀ The room has been restored as closely as possible to match photographs of the original layout taken in 1945. The maps on the walls, for example, were taken from the basement Map Room in the Admiralty. They are almost certainly the same ones used by Churchill in the first few months of the war when he was First Lord of the Admiralty.

▼ The large map on the left-hand wall of the room sports a curious addition. If you trace a line due west from the far north-west tip of Scotland, you will come across this hand-drawn caricature of German leader Adolf Hitler. It is not known when this mocking piece of graffiti was added.

THE MAP ROOM

The Map Room was the nerve centre of Britain's war effort. A week before the war began, a handpicked team of recently retired officers took up their positions at the bank of desks running along the centre of the room. Hours later, the next shift took their place, then the next and the next. It would be six years before the room was left empty again.

Every retreat and advance, every defeat and victory, was recorded in calm, unemotional and faithful detail within this inner sanctum. As one senior member of the War Rooms administrative staff put it: 'Daily truth belonged to the Map Room.'

65

MAP ROOM.

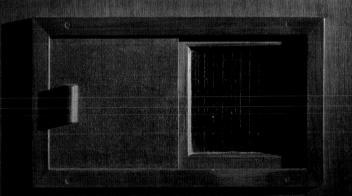

During each shift, five men sat at the desks in the Map Room – one each from the Army, Navy and Air Force, another from the Ministry of Home Security, and a fifth man from each of the services in turn acting as the Duty Officer. It was their job to receive intelligence reports by telephone and on paper, sift through them and then pass on the details to a team of 'plotters' standing ready around the room. They then translated the information on to the maps mounted around the room. In this manner the Map Room acted as something like a scoreboard for the war.

Churchill was a great lover of maps and could often be found in the Map Room, especially when air raids forced the War Cabinet and Defence Committee to meet underground. He took great pleasure in showing the room off to special guests, including the King and Queen in 1942 and General Eisenhower, the Supreme Commander of the Allied Expeditionary Force, in 1944.

Map Room officers at work, c.1945

◀ One of the most important duties of the Map Room staff was to help the Joint Planning staff prepare a daily briefing on the war situation for the Prime Minister, the Chiefs of Staff and the King. This 'CWR Bulletin' was made ready by eight o'clock every morning. As part of the distribution process, one copy was placed in this battered red leather dispatch box. This was then loaded onto a horse-drawn brougham carriage and driven the short distance to Buckingham Palace, where it was brought before the eyes of King George VI.

SUPPLYING THE MAPS

One of the key questions during the setting up of the Map Room was what maps it should contain. It was a difficult question to answer, as Brigadier George Davy explained in a letter to IWM in December 1982:

'War was in sight and [the Deputy Director of Operations at the War Office] asked me if I would stick up the relevant maps in the basement war room... Work space was limited among the concrete and he told me to go and look at it. I did, and when I went back and asked what maps he had in mind, he said: "Your guess is as good as mine." So I went ahead with the "Cockpit of Europe" at the larger scales, smaller for the fringes and tiny for the Far East where there was less certainty of trouble.'

The telephones lined up along the desks were nicknamed the 'beauty chorus' by Map Room staff. The white phones were connected to the War Rooms of each of the three armed services; the green to intelligence sources; and the black to the outside world via a private telephone exchange. It was through these telephones that most information on the war situation was received.

Beside each phone in the Map Room is a switch that allowed incoming calls to be marked by a flashing light rather than a ringing bell. This was presumably a way to maintain calm during especially busy periods.

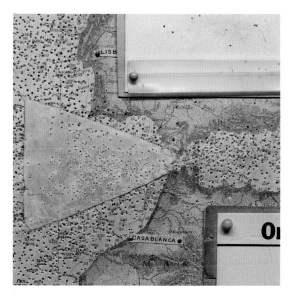

Viewed close-up, it is possible to make out other details on the convoy map, such as sections that became so worn with use that they were replaced; the addition of tags to mark important ports; and faint lines drawn, for example, to denote where Britain's home waters end and the West Atlantic begins.

These sugar cubes belonged to Wing Commander John Heagerty, one of the officers who manned the Map Room from 1939 through to 1945. Sugar was in short supply during the war, and Heagerty appears to have hidden his in an envelope at the back of one of his drawers, where it lay undisturbed until IWM conducted a thorough inventory of the War Rooms in the early 1980s. From the shape of one of the cubes, it looks as if the officer may have conducted his own rationing system, shaving off small amounts of sugar as and when he needed it.

An enormous convoy map dominates one end of the Map Room. Viewed from a distance, it is still possible to see the cloud left behind by tens of thousands of tiny pinholes. Each time a pin was placed in the waters of the North Atlantic or Mediterranean it represented the position of a convoy running the gauntlet of German and Italian submarines to deliver vital supplies to Britain, its allies and its fighting forces. Sometimes it would denote progress, but all too often it would indicate that the ship had been sunk.

EACH PIN POINT
REPRESENTS A CONVOY
MOVEMENT.

Gibraltar

Oran

Algiers

Casablanca

Freetown

Takoradi

Suez

Port Sudan

Aden

Massawa

Addu Atoll

Kilindini

Diego Suarez

Seychelles

Mauritius

Persian Gulf

Bombay

Colombo

INDIAN OCEAN
CONVOY ESCORTS

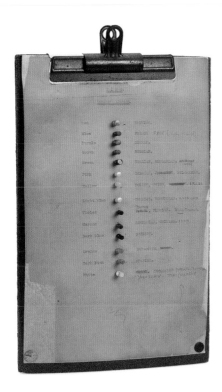

The Map Room in use, 1945

▲ Every pin had a different significance according to its colour. This clipboard, which records the colour-coding used, makes it obvious just how global the Second World War became.

◀ During the Battle of Britain in the summer of 1940, Map Room staff would chalk up on this blackboard the number of enemy aircraft destroyed each day. Later one of the staff painted in these figures from 15 September to create a permanent record of the day that turned the battle decisively in Britain's favour.

THE LURE OF THE MAP ROOM

As Deputy Secretary (Military) to the War Cabinet and Chief of Staff to Churchill, Major-General Hastings Ismay was one of the select few given access to the Map Room. Here he describes why he found it hard to resist going in:

'Whenever a big battle or critical movement was in progress, it was a temptation to find pretexts for going to the [Map Room] at all hours of the day and night, in order to get the latest information. The sensation was not unlike visiting a friend in hospital. One entered the room hoping for the best, but fearing the worst. "How is the Malta convoy going?" one would ask, trying not to appear unduly anxious. The nature of the answer could generally be guessed from the expression of the officer on duty... My visits often coincided with those of a sturdy figure in a siren suit, and I began to understand why my chief was always so embarrassingly up to date with every detail of the situation.'

▶ This was the desk used by the Duty Officer – the Army, Navy or Air Force officer in charge of any given shift in the Map Room. As well as overseeing the work going on in the Map Room, the Duty Officer (alongside the Camp Commandant) was expected to take charge of the defence of the War Rooms if the site came under attack from enemy forces on the ground. Sitting close to the Duty Officer's desk was an ivory telephone, which connected the Map Room to the Prime Minister at 10 Downing Street.

▼ In the Map Room, as everywhere else in the War Rooms, the air would have been thick with cigarette smoke. One letter in the IWM archives describes how a colleague 'always smoked cigarettes' as he studied his maps. 'He used to pore over his contours making calculations and noting the results in countless numbers of extremely small figures ... his face always wreathed in smoke... under the glare of a fluorescent tubular light.'

Myra Murden

BEHIND THE SCENES

The smooth operation of the Map Room depended on many members of staff. One of them was Leading Aircraftwoman Myra Murden:

'I remember sitting and doing short-hand and typing... One night I was just sitting there and waiting and I was drawing a rose... this civilian went by and he said "Right, you can work for us tomorrow." And with that I went... to work for these three draftsmen... They used to do all these huge maps that went down to the Cabinet Room...

'I did the labels and I suppose the grotty jobs, but that didn't worry me... They did all the important secret work on the maps.

'They would put little crosses and things across the Atlantic where U-boats or submarines or ships had been sunk. And it was my job to draw a little submarine and put a little English flag on, or swastika, or a ship on its side...'

▲ When the Map Room officers and clerks arrived at their desks a week before the war began, they found eight boxes waiting for them. Inside them was a 'Massive Reserve Stationery Kit', which was supposed to include everything they would need – from ink bottles like these to envelopes and paperclips. On closer examination, they discovered that it did not contain any coloured card, so this was the one thing they had to do without in the first few days of the war.

This cigarette lighter was rigged up by an electrician during the war. Pressing the button on the right heated a wire filament from which Map Room officers could light their cigarettes. It is thought the device was used to limit the fire hazard presented by naked flames from ordinary cigarette lighters and matches.

S E C R E T   COPY NO. ____

CABINET WAR ROOM RECORD NO. 2074

For the 24 hours ending 0700, 8th May, 1945

1. In accordance with an agreement signed on 7th May, all
German forces in Europe surrendered unconditionally to the
Allies, the "cease-fire" to come into force with effect
from 0001 hours 9th May.

MILITARY

2. Western Europe. The Third U.S. Army has continued to
advance along the DANUBE valley east of LINZ and further north
is sweeping through Western Czechoslovakia on a very wide front.
It is confirmed that PILSEN was captured by U.S. Armoured forces
on the 6th.
        The Second British Army has reached the line of the KIEL
Canal and further west is approaching CUXHAVEN.
        The First Canadian Army has cleared the country between
the WESER and the EMS and occupied EMDEN.

3. Italy. U.S. forces are now stationed alongside New Zealand
and British troops in TRIESTE, where the situation remains quiet.

4. Russian Front. The Russians have reached the River ELBE to
the north and S.E. of MAGDEBURG. They have captured BRESLAU and
made further progress west and S.W. of MORAVSKA OSTRAVA.

AIR

5. Western Front. Yesterday, Allied aircraft dropped 1545 tons
of food supplies in HOLLAND.
        408 fighters (2 missing) provided support for the advance
into CZECHOSLOVAKIA: 2 enemy aircraft were destroyed in combat.

6. French Indo-China. On the 4th, 47 Liberators dropped 91 tons
on the naval dockyard and arsenal at SAIGON. Enemy casualties in
combat 2:3:0.

NAVAL

7. Home Waters. A naval party which has arrived at EMDEN has found
the port apparently in good order. Twenty-five minor warships
are present but no U-boats.

8. Pacific. The British Pacific Fleet has resumed operations
against the SAKISHIMA Islands. Battleships carried out a bombardment
and carrier-borne aircraft attacked airfields. In an attack on
H.M. Carriers by Japanese aircraft, FORMIDABLE was slightly
damaged: 28 aircraft were shot down.

9. Enemy Attack on Shipping.
AVONDALE PARK (2878)   ) sunk by U-boat in coastal convoy
SNELAND ISLAND(1791) Norwegian) off the Firth of Forth yesterday.

Cabinet War Room

8th May, 1945

◀ The Map Room officers helped to produce a daily report which was circulated to the King, Prime Minister, Chiefs of Staff and other officers on every morning of the war. This extract from the report, covering 'the 24 hours ending 0700, 8th May, 1945', shows how victory in Europe was accorded just one short bullet point before the rest of the business of the day followed.

▲ A member of staff highlighted the 'V' on the Map Room clock in red, echoing the 'V' sign used by Winston Churchill to signify Victory.

◀ The date displayed in the Map Room is the day in 1945 that the War Rooms were used for the last time. Japan had surrendered just hours earlier. The war was over.

5

PRESERVING CHURCHILL'S WAR ROOMS

Filed away in the archives of IWM is a small folder containing correspondence between the museum and the government in the months after August 1945. Reading the various letters, memos and notes it is clear that while everyone was quick to recognise the historical value of the War Rooms, there was no clear plan for what should happen to them after the war. There was talk of recreating the Map Room as an exhibit within the museum, and suggestions were made on both sides about specific objects that the museum should acquire – Churchill's chair from the Cabinet Room perhaps and the Convoy Map with its hundreds of thousands of pin holes – but in the end no agreement could be reached.

The only significant step taken by IWM during this period was an arrangement to send a photographer to take a visual record of the site. The images that he captured – some time in either August or September 1945 – show the War Rooms being well looked after. George Rance, the Office of Works employee responsible for the maintenance of the site during the war, can still be seen in attendance, as can several of the Royal Marine orderlies. And all the rooms, though unoccupied by staff, are pictured still ready for use – from the Churchills' dining room to the Officers' Mess.

In the year after the photographs were taken, large sections of the site were stripped out and returned to general government use. Only a handful of rooms were left untouched – the Map Room and its annexe, the Transatlantic Telephone Room, the Cabinet Room and Churchill's bedroom. One motivating factor for the temporary preservation of these rooms was the level of interest shown in them by the public. In September 1946 Lawrence Burgis, one of the Cabinet Office officials who had helped to set up the War Rooms, wrote:

> I have been astonished at the amount of interest
> shown in the CWR by the outside public and such

Ismay and Rance show journalists the Map Room, March 1948

like and have always given them every facility to visit the place... And of course Mr Rance is a marvellous guide.

It appears then that groups of visitors were already being given unofficial tours of the rooms at this very early stage. More remarkably still, the preserved rooms still contained a great many top secret documents. It was only thought wise to remove these in November 1947.

The level of public interest grew so great that it was decided to put the preservation of the rooms on a more official basis. This decision was announced in Parliament early in 1948, and a press conference was held in the War Rooms themselves on 17 March. Photographs of this occasion can be found in the IWM archive, showing Ismay and Rance making a presentation to journalists and then leading them on a tour of the rooms. It was a tour that Rance would continue to lead for other groups until 1950, when ill-health forced him to step down at the age of 76. A retired Royal Marine took his place.

During the 1950s and 1960s – as the Cold War reached its height – members of the public visiting the War Rooms would have been astonished to discover that secret work was still being carried out just yards away from where they were standing. Rooms 62, 62A and 62B, for example, were adapted for use by the Chiefs of Staff to serve as a conference room, teleprinter room and cypher room, and the whole complex was earmarked to act as 'Quarters for the central Government in the event of an emergency'. Indeed, documents in the IWM archive suggest that a command centre

was re-established in the War Rooms during the Suez Crisis of 1956. Chief among them is a letter (shown overleaf) received in November 1956 by former Map Room officer Wing Commander John Heagerty. It came from a former colleague, Air Marshal William Dickson, who wrote:

> We opened up the CWR for our little war in the Middle East. It was humming with activity all down the corridor and the old mess at the end of the corridor was revived and the famous green tin cupboard in the corner restocked with drink... We did not touch your old map room, which is still there as a museum, but made another one out of the rooms nearer the mess. All of this brought 1939-45 back vividly to memory. We even issued the daily CWR Summary to Ministers on the famous paper.

Another document in the Ministry of Defence archives reveals that in 1961 the Chiefs of Staff wanted to reclaim at least part of the area being shown to visitors. The idea was 'to establish a War Room manned permanently on a skeleton basis', but it does not seem to have come to fruition.

By the 1970s almost 5,000 visitors were touring the rooms every year. There was no set route for this tour; visitors were simply escorted into each room in turn and allowed to look around as the mood took them. In 1974 one member of IWM staff noted with a certain amount of disapproval: 'It is quite normal for visitors to bounce up and down on the Prime Minister's bed, to sit in his chair and look into the drawers of his desk.'

Concerns were also growing about the state of the rooms themselves, where the dry and dusty conditions were taking their toll on less durable items such as soft furnishings and documents. The government eventually decided to spend £7,000 on conservation work, but also began looking for ways to recoup these costs and make the site more self-sustaining. One idea was to open up the War Rooms to more visitors and to charge them a fee for entry. There were certainly plenty of people keen to see the site – every year the Cabinet Office received applications from 30,000 to 40,000 potential visitors, but had to turn the vast majority away.

In 1974, IWM was asked to take on the project. On one level it was an extremely attractive prospect, especially to the museum's then Director-General Dr Noble Frankland, who had spent several years in the War Rooms after the war working on an official history of Bomber Command. Eventually, however, the museum's trustees decided to turn down the opportunity, citing the financial commitments it already had to its new branch at Duxford, which opened in 1976, and HMS *Belfast* in 1978.

The question was posed again in 1981 – this time with the personal backing of Prime Minister Margaret Thatcher. Negotiations were held with the National Trust and Madame Tussauds, but IWM remained the government's preferred choice. In January 1982 the museum duly agreed to take over the management of the site, on the condition that the Department of the Environment pay for the setting-up costs. The scene was now set for two years of extraordinary work, preserving the key rooms that had been open to the public since the end of the war, and restoring over a

dozen more to their wartime appearance.

To begin with the plan was to stick to the tried and tested procedure of escorting small groups of visitors in and out of the rooms, so preserving the original structure and layout of the site. Eventually, however, it was decided to create a one-way route for visitors to circulate around unescorted, and to glaze off the rooms so that they could be viewed without being entered. Before any structural work could take place, the contents of the rooms had to be catalogued and removed for conservation and storage elsewhere. Copies of this original inventory are still held by IWM. Room by room, object by object, some 7,000 items were numbered, described and measured, and their locations recorded in painstaking detail. Take, for example, object number E69B-3-3 in the War Cabinet Room. It is a paper knife with sheath and rubber, measuring 19cm in length, positioned 10cm from the front edge of the table and 145cm from the edge of the table closest to 'Wall I'. It was there when IWM took over the site in 1982, and it was back in the exact same position when restoration work on the rooms was complete.

Much of the structural work on the site involved creating openings in the existing fabric of the building to allow visitors to see into the rooms and to provide a straightforward one-way route to move around the building. Between Room 62B and the Map Room Annexe this involved drilling a passageway through a chamber that had been filled with concrete to strengthen the site during the war. The job was expected to take about three weeks to complete, but such was the quality of the concrete that it took three months.

MINISTRY OF DEFENCE,

STOREY'S GATE,

S.W.1.

22nd November, 1956.

Dear John,

Many thanks for your letter of 5th November, 1956, which I should have answered before but overlooked in the rush. I am very sorry indeed to have to reply that I cannot come to the C.W.R. dinner next Tuesday. My excuse is a good one because that night I am dining with the Queen and the Army Council!

Please remember me to all my old friends. You may like to tell them that we opened up the C.W.R. for our little war in the Middle East. It was humming with activity all down the corridor and the old mess at the end of the corridor was revived and the famous green tin cupboard in the corner restocked with drink. They even had one of the old Marines back again (I forget his name). We did not touch your old map room, which is still there as a museum, but made another one out of one of the rooms nearer the mess. All this brought 1939/45 back vividly to memory. We even issued the daily C.W.R. Summary to Ministers on the famous paper.

Best wishes for a very happy reunion.

Yours ever,

Diki.

P.S.   I am fully fit again, thank you.

Wing Commander J. Heagerty,
    36, Walpole Street,
        Chelsea,
            London, S.W.3.

There were other challenges too: the adaptation of the wartime ventilation trunking to allow for two separate ventilation systems (one for the public areas, one to create a stringently controlled atmosphere to protect the contents of the sealed rooms); the rewiring of the site while retaining all of the original lamps and fittings; and the careful cleaning of the rooms to restore them to their wartime appearance.

While all of this work was going on, IWM historians Peter Simkins, Mike Houlihan and Jon Wenzel were hard at work piecing together the story of the War Rooms – no easy task given that the site was constructed, developed and operated in such secrecy. They were ably assisted by Nigel de Lee, who was then a teacher at the Royal Military Academy, Sandhurst. It was his role to delve deeply into the government's archives to uncover the key decisions and correspondence that underpinned every aspect of the site's history.

Simkins, Houlihan and Wenzel built on de Lee's factual foundations by trawling through the papers, diaries and autobiographies of the main players in the War Rooms story, including Churchill, Ismay, Hollis, Alanbrooke and Bridges – all of whom had died before the restoration process began. They conducted interviews with the few surviving senior staff such as Sir John Colville and Sir John Winnifrith (establishment officer of the War Cabinet Office), and consulted the far greater number of surviving junior officers, secretaries and personal assistants, most of whom had of course been much younger during their wartime service.

All of this research helped the historians establish the facts of how the War Rooms were used at different points during the war. It was a messy story, with many of the rooms being divided and sub-divided and their uses changing as Britain's wartime priorities evolved. It was therefore decided to restore the rooms to look as they would have done during their 'period of maximum use', which by and large boiled down to the months between the end of the Battle of France in summer 1940 and the end of the Blitz in spring 1941.

It fell to Jon Wenzel, who was to become the first curator of the War Rooms, to source all the furniture, fixtures and fittings required to make the reconstruction of the rooms as accurate as possible. Fortunately, all of the furniture used in the site turned out to have been standardised (with the exception of the Prime Minister's room), and Wenzel was able to source much of it by submitting regular 'shopping lists' to the furniture clearing warehouse run by the government's Property Services Agency. He was also given access to different government departments to look for typewriters, chairs and wicker baskets that had managed to remain part of civil service life since the 1940s.

The decision was also made to include Tussaud-like waxworks to give a better impression of the rooms in use. The creation of these figures was subject to a great deal of care and attention. Volunteers were brought in to assume particular positions and then casts were made from which the mannequins were constructed. Their poses were chosen to add a sense of movement to the rooms. One officer is shown searching for something in a cupboard, but look more closely and you can see that the phone on his desk is off the

Margaret Thatcher is given a tour of the site after formally opening the War Rooms, 4 April 1984

hook – someone on the other end of the line is clearly waiting for him to find the right document. Finally came the display panels, audio-guides and guidebooks that would help visitors gain a full understanding not only of what the War Rooms were for, but also what it was like to work there. Here the input of former War Rooms staff was especially invaluable, with their insights, impressions and anecdotes bringing the site to life for generations of visitors.

On 4 April 1984 many of those staff members were in attendance – alongside members of Churchill's family – when the War Rooms were formally opened to the public by Prime Minister Margaret Thatcher. Two days later at 10.00am the first paying visitor, Mrs C Hockenhull, was welcomed by Jon Wenzel and asked to sign the Cabinet War Rooms visitors' book.

Over the next few years hundreds of thousands of visitors flocked to the site, more than vindicating the decision to open it up to the public. Nonetheless, only a third of the original basement site was accessible for viewing – measuring little more than 1,000 square metres. During wartime many more rooms had been in use, which had since been stripped out and returned to general government use. Some became little more than casual dumping grounds for the government offices above, and one room was even converted to a gym. In 1993 there came a new director for the War Rooms in the shape of Phil Reed, who began pressing for these other sections of the basement to be made available to IWM. By 2001, he had successfully secured access to an additional area of over 2,000 square metres, and work began to put it to use.

The first section to be opened up in 2003 included the so-called Churchill Suite, containing the rooms originally set aside for the Prime Minister and his family and entourage. The photographs taken of the site back in 1945 proved to be a vital resource as museum staff set about locating the fixtures, fittings and furniture necessary for the restoration. The search took them through old government offices and second-hand shops, and even to the house at Windsor Great Park once occupied by Queen Elizabeth, the Queen Mother, where a plate-warmer was found to match the one used in the Churchills' kitchen.

Other sections of the basement were converted into an education facility, conference centre and cafe for the site, but the largest space was set aside to become the Churchill Museum – designed to tell the story of the wartime Prime Minister's remarkable 90-year life. Opened in 2005, 60 years after the end of the war and 40 years after Churchill's death, the museum is a superb modern counterpart to the preserved wartime rooms. Its centrepiece is the Churchill Lifeline – a 15-metre-long, electronic table that acts as an interactive timeline of Sir Winston's life. Visitors can use a touch strip along the side of the table to scroll through Churchill's life year by year and even day by day, and they can also pull up thousands of documents, images, animations and films to bring different parts of his story to life.

The addition of the Churchill Museum has breathed new life into the War Rooms, with visitor numbers consistently climbing. Over 75 years after the Second World War, the remarkable story of Churchill and his War Rooms – so carefully preserved and restored by IWM – continues to captivate and enthral.

About the author

Jonathan Asbury is the author of the official Churchill War Rooms guidebook, as well as guidebooks for HMS Belfast, IWM London, IWM North and IWM Duxford. He is a graduate of Churchill College, Cambridge – founded in honour of the wartime Prime Minister – and has enjoyed a life-long fascination with the way that the Second World War was won.

Acknowledgements

I had just finished writing a new visitor's guidebook for Churchill War Rooms when I was asked to provide the text for this more in-depth volume. Inevitably that new guidebook leant heavily on its predecessors, especially the first and most comprehensive of them (known as 'the bible' by present-day IWM staff). Produced in readiness for the opening of the War Rooms to the public in 1984, its author was Peter Simkins, one of IWM's in-house historians, who played a major role in the preservation and restoration of the site.

Simkins in turn relied on an unpublished history of the War Rooms, prepared by Nigel de Lee from the Royal Military Academy, Sandhurst. This history, which survives as a manuscript in the IWM archives, is an invaluable resource, based on a meticulous examination of government records and other primary source material. It is on de Lee's scholarly work that all subsequent histories of the War Rooms rely.

IWM also used de Lee's work as the factual foundation for the physical restoration of the site – determining as far as possible the precise function of each room, who worked where, and how the use of the basement evolved during the war. But the IWM team needed more. They needed to know the telling details: how particular rooms were set out, what ad-hoc arrangements were made that were never recorded in official government documents and, most importantly, what it felt like to be here on a day-to-day basis. They needed to talk to the people who knew the War Rooms best – the men and women who worked, ate and slept here as bombs rained down on the streets above.

Two other IWM historians, Mike Houlihan and Jon Wenzel, worked alongside Simkins and de Lee to track down, correspond with and talk to a wide range of War Rooms veterans, drawing out the kind of insights and stories that have since brought the site back to life. As a result of this research, IWM now has an extraordinary archive of personal papers and audio interviews, which has proved to be a crucial resource in putting together this book. (It was especially useful, for example, to see a donated copy of the Standing Instructions for the War Rooms – a document communicating all the mundane details that staff needed to know.)

Some of the IWM team's original notes and memos have also survived, stored in filing cabinets behind the scenes at the War Rooms. When I first began research on this book, Phil Reed, the outgoing Director of Churchill War Rooms, kindly allowed me access to these files, which include the meticulous inventory taken when IWM took over the site in the early 1980s, and other fascinating nuggets such as a BBC engineer's description of how Churchill's radio broadcasts from the basement were arranged. Phil Reed himself proved to be an outstanding source of information and inspiration, regaling me with anecdotes from his thirteen years in charge of the site and treating me to a personal tour of some of the key rooms – the excitement of which I have tried to capture in this book. His love for the underground complex was evident and infectious, and his knowledge of the site is unsurpassed. Future historians would do well to capture more of his expertise on paper or as part of IWM's own audio archive.

Of course, not all of our understanding of the War Rooms comes from IWM's archives. First-hand insight into the site's inner workings began to emerge in the decades after the war – in the memoirs and diaries of key players such as General Lord Ismay, General Sir Leslie Hollis, Field Marshal Lord Alanbrooke, John Colville, Elizabeth Nel, Joan Bright Astley and, of course, Churchill himself. I also owe a profound debt to two excellent works of history: Churchill's Bunker, in which Professor Richard Holmes weaves together

a masterly account of life in the secret headquarters; and Roy Jenkins' superb biography of Churchill, which I found an immensely valuable guide to the broader context of the war.

Working on this book has been a privilege. I would like to thank Liz Bowers and David Fenton of IWM for asking me to get involved, former director of Churchill War Rooms Phil Reed for his generosity and support, exhibitions manager Lucy Tindle for helping with the photo shoots, Ian Kikuchi and Lucy Tindle again for casting their expert eyes over the text, Andrew Tunnard for his superb photography and readiness to pitch in, Stephen Long for working his design alchemy on a trickily constructed manuscript, and Madeleine James and the rest of the publishing team at IWM for guiding me so patiently along the way.

I would also like to thank my mum and dad for their continuing love and support, George, Herbie, Iris, Connie and Martha for sparing me a few hours here and there to get on with writing this book, and Kathryn whose steadfast love, understanding and friendship has made it possible for me to pursue what the Chinese might call an 'interesting' career.

Sources

Bibliography

Alanbrooke, Field Marshal Lord (ed. Alex Danchev and Daniel Todman), War Diaries 1939–45 (1992) © The Estate of Field Marshal Alan Francis Brooke, 1st Viscount Alanbrooke

Astley, Joan Bright, The Inner Circle. A View of the War at the Top (1971)

© The Estate of Joan Bright Astley

Churchill, Winston, The Complete Speeches Volume VI (1974)

Reproduced with permission of Curtis Brown, London, on behalf of The Estate of Winston S. Churchill. © The Estate of Winston S. Churchill

Churchill, Winston, The Second World War (1948–53)

Reproduced with permission of Curtis Brown, London, on behalf of The Estate of Winston S. Churchill. © The Estate of Winston S. Churchill

Colville, John, The Fringes of Power: Downing Street Diaries 1939-55 (1985)

© The Estate of Sir John Colville

de Lee, Nigel, History of the Cabinet War Rooms 1939-45 (unpublished manuscript c.1983)

Finch, Cressida, A Short History of the Cabinet War Rooms 1945-84, (article for Despatches: The Magazine of the Friends of IWM, summer 2009)

Gilbert, Martin, Winston S. Churchill, Vol. 6, Finest Hour 1939–41 (1983)

– Winston S. Churchill, Vol.7, Road to Victory 1941-45 (1986)

Hickman, Tom, Churchill's Bodyguard (2008)

Hollis, General Sir Leslie, One Marine's Tale (1956) © The Estate of General Sir Leslie Hollis

Holmes, Richard, Churchill's Bunker. The Secret Headquarters at the Heart of Britain's Victory (2009)

Ismay, General Lord, Memoirs (1960)

© The Estate of General Lord Hastings Ismay, 1st Baron Ismay

Jenkins, Roy, Churchill (2002)

Leasor, James, War at the Top (1959)

Moody, Joanna, From Churchill's War Rooms. Letters of a Secretary 1943-45 (2007)

Nel, Elizabeth, Winston Churchill by his Private Secretary (2007 ed.)

Nicolson, Harold, Letters and Diaries, 1939-45 (1966) © The Estate of Sir Harold Nicolson

Sandys, Celia, Churchill (2013 ed.)

Simkins, Peter, Cabinet War Rooms (1983)

Singer, Barry, Churchill Style (2012)

Soames, Mary, A Daughter's Tale (2012) © The Estate of Mary Soames

Soames, Mary (ed), Speaking for Themselves (1999)

Clementine Spencer-Churchill quotations reproduced with permission of Churchill Archives Centre, Churchill College.

Thompson, Walter H, I Was Churchill's Shadow (1951) © The Estate of Walter H Thompson

IWM Audio Archive

3168, Air Vice Marshal Sir William Dickson

6191, Lieutenant-General Sir Ian Jacob

6356, Sir John Winnifrith

6380, Sir John Colville

6858, Stephen Geis © Stephen M Geis

9539, Frank Higgins

12441, Joint Planning officer Alan Melville

15119, Elizabeth Nel (née Layton)

18162, Joint Planning officer David Lee

18163, Ilene Adams (née Hutchinson) © Ilene Hutchinson

19836, Joan Bright-Astley

23845, Leading Aircraftwoman Myra Collyer (née Murden)

31053, Aircraftswoman Rachel Foster

33037, Patrick Kinna

Private papers lodged with IWM

Lieutenant Colonel E N Buxton

18163 Ilene Adams (nee Hutchinson)

Documents.2773 General Sir Leslie Hollis

Documents.2995 Wing Commander John Heagerty

There are also files of miscellaneous papers relating to the War Rooms, including items such as the Standing Instructions for staff.

Filed correspondence between IWM and CWR staff

Brigadier Davy

Captain Ray Edghill

© The Estate of Captain Ray Edghill

Mrs Margaret d'Arcy

Mr H J Gregory

There are also copies of the inventory taken when IWM took over the site in the early 1980s, as well as countless other useful memos and reports.

Quotations by Winston Churchill reproduced with permission of Curtis Brown, London, on behalf of The Estate of Winston S. Churchill. © The Estate of Winston S. Churchill

Image List

All images © IWM unless otherwise stated. Every effort has been made to contact all copyright holders. The publishers will be glad to make good in future editions any error or omissions brought to their attention.

Chapter 1

MH 27616; COL 30; © Shutterstock.com; MH 520; IWM 18163; Documents.2995; IWM_SITE_CWR_186; MH 534; IWM_SITE_CWR_188; CWR_1824; IWM 3444; Documents_017438_A_1; IWM_SITE_CWR_000617; IWM_SITE_CWR_000619; IWM_SITE_CWR_000618; IWM_SITE_CWR_000620; IWM_SITE_CWR_000616; IWM_SITE_CWR_000110; IWM_SITE_CWR_000615; IWM_SITE_CWR_000621; IWM_SITE_CWR_000660; IWM_SITE_CWR_000661; IWM_SITE_CWR_000663; IWM_SITE_CWR_000472; IWM_SITE_CWR_000593; A_030046_Ismay; IWM_SITE_CWR_000588; MH_000524; IWM_SITE_CWR_000587; IWM_SITE_CWR_000591; IWM_SITE_CWR_000500; IWM_SITE_CWR_000062; IWM_SITE_CWR_000060

Chapter 2

H_3978; HU_45910; HU_45913; IWM_SITE_CWR_000464; IWM_SITE_CWR_000468; IWM_SITE_CWR_000103; IWM 15119; IWM_SITE_CWR_000461; MH_000533; IWM_SITE_CWR_000623; IWM_SITE_CWR_000603; IWM_SITE_CWR_000605; IWM_SITE_CWR_000607; IWM_SITE_CWR_000583; IWM_SITE_CWR_000585; FEQ_000864; NYF_019390; IWM_SITE_CWR_000496; IWM_SITE_CWR_000497; IWM_SITE_CWR_000652; IWM_SITE_CWR_000449; IWM_SITE_CWR_000649; IWM_SITE_CWR_000654; IWM_SITE_CWR_000653; IWM_SITE_CWR_000580 & CWR_002059; CWR_002056; IWM_SITE_CWR_000509; IWM_SITE_CWR_000508; IWM_SITE_CWR_000675; IWM_SITE_CWR_000669; IWM_SITE_CWR_000448; MH_000538; IWM_SITE_CWR_000637; IWM_SITE_CWR_000499; IWM_SITE_CWR_000632; IWM_SITE_CWR_000633; IWM_SITE_CWR_000631; IWM_SITE_CWR_000636;

Chapter 3

E_18980; A_18749; IWM_SITE_CWR_000639; IWM_SITE_CWR_000638; H_16478; IWM_SITE_CWR_000566; HU_043546; IWM_SITE_CWR_000561; IWM_SITE_CWR_000563; IWM_SITE_CWR_000564; IWM_SITE_CWR_000642; IWM_SITE_CWR_000643; IWM_SITE_CWR_000645; IWM_SITE_CWR_000647; IWM_SITE_CWR_000484; IWM_SITE_CWR_000648; IWM_SITE_CWR_000640; H_3512 IWM_SITE_CWR_000664; IWM_SITE_CWR_000666; IWM_SITE_CWR_000665; CWR_002058; IWM_SITE_CWR_000614; Documents_009180_A_1; IWM_SITE_CWR_000111; IWM_SITE_CWR_000613; IWM_SITE_CWR_000598; IWM_SITE_CWR_000672; HU_045346 Courtesy of National Security Agency of the Department of Defence, USA; IWM_SITE_CWR_000670; IWM_SITE_CWR_000671; IWM_SITE_CWR_000673

Chapter 4

HU 55965; IWM_SITE_CWR_000626; HU_103536 © National Portrait Gallery, London; HU_043777; IWM_SITE_CWR_000624; IWM0018; Documents_009858_A_1; IWM_SITE_CWR_000106; IWM_SITE_CWR_000553; IWM_SITE_CWR_000552; IWM_SITE_CWR_000456; IWM_SITE_CWR_000556; IWM_SITE_CWR_000579; HU_058517; IWM_SITE_CWR_000567; CWR_000406; IWM_SITE_CWR_000575; IWM_SITE_CWR_000573; IWM_SITE_CWR_000570; MAP_DETAIL_1; CWR_000389_1; IWM_SITE_CWR_000674; CWR_001890; HU_074904; CWR_000504; IWM_SITE_CWR_000572; Documents_25644 © Mrs Myra N Collyer (nee Murden); CWR_000788; CWR_001895_1; Documents_002995_C; CWR_001896; CWR_001894

Chapter 5

MH_27624; HeagertyJS_002995_4; IWM_1984_015_120